CSLI
Lecture Notes
Number 81

COMPUTING NATURAL LANGUAGE

edited by
**Atocha Aliseda
Rob van Glabbeek
Dag Westerståhl**

CSLI PUBLICATIONS

CENTER FOR THE STUDY OF
LANGUAGE AND INFORMATION
STANFORD, CALIFORNIA

Copyright © 1998
CSLI Publications
Center for the Study of Language and Information
Leland Stanford Junior University
Printed in the United States
02 01 00 99 98   5 4 3 2 1

Library of Congress Cataloging-in-Publication Data

Computing natural language / edited by Atocha Aliseda, Rob van Glabbeek,
and Dag Westerståhl.
p.   cm. — (CSLI lecture notes ; no. 81)
This vol. is an outgrowth of the Fourth CSLI Workshop on Logic, Language,
and Computation, held at the Center for the Study of Language and
Information (CSLI) at Stanford University, June 2–4, 1995.
"Center for the Study of Language and Information."
Includes bibliographical references and index.

ISBN 1-57586-101-1 (hardback : alk. paper).
ISBN 1-57586-100-3 (pbk. : alk. paper)

1. Computational linguistics. I. Aliseda, Atocha. II. Van Glabbeek, Rob J.
III. Westerståhl, Dag, 1946–   . IV. CSLI Workshop on Logic, Language, and
Computation (4th : 1995) V. Center for the Study of Language and
Information (U.S.) VI. Series.
P98.C619   1998
410′.285—dc21   97-43831
CIP

∞ The acid-free paper used in this book meets the minimum requirements of
the American National Standard for Information Sciences—Permanence of
Paper for Printed Library Materials, ANSI Z39.48-1984.

CSLI was founded early in 1983 by researchers from Stanford University, SRI
International, and Xerox PARC to further research and development of integrated
theories of language, information, and computation. CSLI headquarters and CSLI
Publications are located on the campus of Stanford University.
CSLI Publications reports new developments in the study of language, information,
and computation. In addition to lecture notes, our publications include
monographs, working papers, revised dissertations, and conference proceedings. Our
aim is to make new results, ideas, and approaches available as quickly as possible.
Please visit our web site at
http://csli-www.stanford.edu/publications/
for comments on this and other titles, as well as for changes and corrections by the
author and publisher.

Contents

Preface

Research at the interface of logic, language, and computation has been fruitful since the seventies. Indeed, the last few years have shown an increasing interest is this field. Amongst the many contributions witnessing this trend are the predecessors to this current volume: *Dynamics, Polarity, and Quantification*, edited by Kanazawa and Piñón, and *Quantifiers, Deduction, and Context*, edited by Kanazawa, Piñón, and De Swart.

Following the tradition established in these volumes, this book pursues the same themes—as expressed by their titles—and adds connections to artificial intelligence and machine learning. It contains a variety of contributions to the logical and computational analysis of natural language. A wide range of logical and computational tools are employed, and applied to such varied areas as context-dependency, linguistic discourse, and formal grammar.

The papers by Perry and McCarthy & Buvač are concerned with contextual dynamics. The former addresses mechanisms of reference in natural language, proposing a classification of indexicals, according to their dependency on context. The latter introduces contexts as formal objects, and proposes a theory for lifting assertions from one context to another. Although these contributions come from different traditions— philosophy and artificial intelligence—van Benthem's paper comments on both, discussing common points from the perspective of modal and first-order logic, and sketching a two-level context formalism.

Jaspars and Kameyama present a logical basis for an integrated model of discourse semantics and pragmatics, by combining dynamic semantics in linguistics and preferential reasoning in AI within a dynamic modal logic setting. They show how this framework can be used to analyze preferential resolution of ambiguous pronouns in discourse.

Sánchez-Valencia discusses the semantics of negative polarity items (e.g., *any*, *ever*) triggered by affective predicates (e.g., *inconceivable*, *unlikely*). By treating these predicates as *gradable* he shows that they are downward monotone expressions, fitting Ladusaw's hypothesis.

Moshier proposes a novel type-theoretic view of Head-Driven Phrase Structure Grammar, and shows how some of its principles and definitions are special cases of a common category-theoretic notion of universality. This approach solves certain problems with the status of lexical entries and lexical rules within a grammar.

Finally, Suppes, Böttner & Liang present a theory of machine learning of natural language, based on a number of learning axioms, which they apply to physics word problems.

Like its predecessors, the present volume is an outgrowth, but by no means a faithful representation of, the FOURTH CSLI WORKSHOP ON LOGIC, LANGUAGE, AND COMPUTATION, which was held at the Center for the Study of Language and Information (CSLI) at Stanford University on June 2–4, 1995. The workshop was organized by Johan van Benthem, Stanley Peters, Atocha Aliseda and Yookyung Kim. Financial support was provided by the School of Humanities and Sciences, CSLI, the Department of Linguistics, the Department of Philosophy, the HPSG project, and Professor Vaughan Pratt. This support is gratefully acknowledged.

Atocha Aliseda
Rob van Glabbeek
Dag Westerståhl

Contributors

JOHAN VAN BENTHEM is Professor of Logic at the University of Amsterdam (Department of Mathematics and Computer Science), and Bonsall Visiting Professor at Stanford University (Department of Philosophy). His research interests include mathematics of modal logics, interfaces between logic and natural language, and logical theories of cognitive actions.

MICHAEL BÖTTNER is a visiting scholar from the Max Planck Institute of Psycholinguistics at Nijmegen. His current interests are procedural semantics, language and space, and language learning.

SAŠA BUVAČ is writing a Ph.D. thesis on formalizing context, at the Computer Science Department of Stanford University.

JAN JASPARS is a free-lance logician. He received a Ph.D. from the former institute of artificial intelligence and language technology (ITK), Tilburg, The Netherlands. His main research interest is applied modal logic.

LIN LIANG received his Ph.D. from Stanford University and was a research associate at the Center for the Study of Language and Information of Stanford University. His research focuses on machine learning of natural languages.

MEGUMI KAMEYAMA is a senior computer scientist at the Artificial Intelligence Center of SRI International in Menlo Park, California. She received a Ph.D. in linguistics and an M.S.C.S in computer science from Stanford University. Her research areas are computational discourse models, logical theory of discourse pragmatics, grammar-pragmatics interface, information extraction, and machine translation.

JOHN MCCARTHY is Professor of Computer Science at Stanford University. He has been interested in artificial intelligence since 1948 and coined the term in 1955. His main artificial intelligence research area has been the formalization of common sense knowledge. He invented the LISP programming language in 1958, developed the concept of time-sharing in the late fifties and early sixties, and has worked on proving that computer programs meet their specifications since the early sixties. He invented the circumscription method of non-monotonic reasoning in 1978. His main research at present is formalizing common sense knowledge and reasoning.

M. Andrew Moshier is assistant professor in computer science and mathematics at Chapman University in Orange, California. His interests include mathematical foundations of theoretical linguistics, proof theoretic approaches to domain theory, and simulation of large-scale, component-based physical systems.

John Perry is the H.W. Stuart Professor of Philosophy at Stanford and Director of the Center for the Study of Language and Information. His work focusses on philosophical problems about reference, meaning, and the self and philosophical issues related to disabilities.

Víctor Sánchez-Valencia received his Ph.D. from ILLC. He is assistant professor at the University of Groningen. His research interests include natural language semantics, categorial grammar and the history of logic, in particular the medieval period.

Patrick Suppes is Lucie Stern Professor of Philosophy Emeritus at Stanford University. His current research interests are machine learning of natural language, with emphasis on robotic language and physics word problems; brain-wave recognition of words and sentences, using EEG and MEG recordings; computer-based distant learning of mathematics and physics.

1

Indexicals, Contexts and Unarticulated Constituents

JOHN PERRY

Philosophers and logicians use the term "indexical" for words such as "I", "you" and "tomorrow". Demonstratives such as "this" and "that" and demonstrative phrases such as "this man" and "that computer" are usually reckoned as a subcategory of indexicals. (Following Kaplan 1989.) The "context-dependence" of indexicals is often taken as a defining feature: what an indexical designates *shifts* from context to context. But there are many kinds of shiftiness, with corresponding conceptions of context. Until we clarify what we mean by "context", this defining feature remains unclear. In sections 1–3, which are largely drawn from Perry 1997a, I try to clarify the sense in which indexicals are context-dependent and make some distinctions among the ways indexicals depend on context. In sections 3–6, I contrast indexicality with another phenomenon that I call "unarticulated constituents."

1 Presemantic Uses of Context

Sometimes we use context to figure out with which meaning a word is being used, or which of several words that look or sound alike is being used, or even which language is being spoken. These are *presemantic* uses of context. I will contrast them with indexicals and anaphora, where context is used *semantically*.

Consider this utterance:

(1) Ich! (said by several teenagers at camp in response to the question, "Who would like some sauerkraut?").

Knowing that this happened in Frankfurt rather than San Francisco might help us determine that it was German teenagers expressing en-

Computing Natural Language.
Atocha Aliseda, Rob van Glabbeek, and Dag Westerståhl, editors.

thusiasm and not American teenagers expressing disgust. In this case context is relevant to figuring out which language (and hence which word with which meaning) is being used.

The vocable "ich" is a *homonym* across languages. Homonyms are words that are spelled and pronounced alike. For example, there are two words in English that are spelled and pronounced "quail"; one is a noun that stands for a small game bird, the other a verb for faltering or recoiling in terror. It makes sense to speak of two words that are pronounced and spelled the same, because words are not merely patterns of sound or combinations of letters, but cultural objects with histories; our two words "quail" derived from different French and Latin words. The term "vocable" can be used for what the words have in common, so if we need to be precise we can say the vocable "quail" corresponds to two words in English.

Each of the German teen-agers, when they use the indexical "ich," designates herself, and so the expression "ich" designates differently for each of them. One might be tempted to consider this just more homonymity. Each has a different name for himself or herself, they just happen to all be spelled alike and sound alike; we have homonyms across idiolects of the same language. Such a temptation should surely be resisted as an explanation of the shiftiness of indexicals. For one thing, the word "ich" doesn't have different historical origins depending on which teen-ager uses it; they all learned the standard first-person in German. The homonym account would be even worse for temporal and spatial indexicals. We would have to suppose that I use a different word "tomorrow" each day, since my use of "tomorrow" shifts its designation every night at the stroke of midnight.

An *ambiguous* expression like "bank" may designate one kind of thing when you say "Where's a good bank?" while worried about finances, another when I use it, thinking about fishing.[1] Its designation varies with different uses, because different of its meanings are relevant. Again, all sorts of contextual facts may be relevant to helping us determine this. Is the speaker holding a wad of money or a fishing pole? It isn't always simply the meaning of a particular word that is in question, and sometimes questions of meaning, syntax and the identity of the words go together:

(2) I forgot how good beer tastes.[2]

---

[1] Let's assume that there is but a single word here, both of the meanings in question deriving from an original meaning of a raised shelf, natural or artificial. That is an oversimpification of the whole story.

[2] Thanks to Ivan Sag for the examples.

(3) I saw her duck under the table.

With (2), knowing whether our speaker has just arrived from Germany or just arrived from Saudi Arabia might help us to decide what the syntactic structure of the sentence is and whether "good" was being used as an adjective or an adverb.

Is "duck" a noun or a verb in (3)? In this case, knowing a little about the situation that this utterance is describing will help us to decide whether the person in question had lost her pet or was seeking security in an earthquake.

2   Semantic Uses of Context

In cases of homonymity and ambiguity the context, the environment of the utterance, the larger situation in which it occurs, helps us to determine what is said. In these cases it is a sort of accident, external to the utterance, that context is needed. We need the context to identify which name, syntactic structure or meaning is used because the very same shapes and sounds happen to be shared by other words, structures, or meanings.

The case of indexicals and anaphors is quite different. We still need context *after* we determine which words, syntactic structures and meanings are being used. The meanings *exploit* the context to perform their function.

In the case of anaphora, the contextual facts have to do with the relation of the utterance to previous nouns in the discourse. In the case of indexicals and demonstratives, rather different sorts of facts are relevant, having to do with the relation of the utterance to things other than words, such as the speaker, addressee, time and place of the utterance. Consider, for example "That man came to see me yesterday. He is interested in philosophy." Resolving the reference of "he" involves knowing two sorts of facts. First, one must know that the use of "he" is anaphorically related to "that man". Second, one must know at which man the utterance context of "that man" was directed.

We use the third-person pronouns "he" and "she" both anaphorically and demonstratively:

(4) A woman wrote a very interesting dissertation at UCLA. She advocated subjective semantics.

(5) (Indicating a certain woman) She advocated subjective semantics in her UCLA dissertation.

How should we treat the occurrences of "she" in (4) and (5)? No one supposes they are mere homonyms. Many philosophers are at least tempted to suppose they are occurrences of a single ambiguous word, which sometimes functions as a variable and sometimes as an indexical (Kaplan 1989). Many linguists find this implausible, and would prefer an account that gives a uniform treatment of pronouns, bringing the relativity to linguistic and other contextual factors into a single framework for a subject matter called "deixis" (Partee 1989, Condoravdi and Gawron 1996). I have some sympathy with this point of view, but for the purposes of this essay I will set the issue of the precise connection of anaphoric and demonstrative uses of pronouns to one side.

3   Types of indexical contexts

With respect to contexts for indexicals, I want to emphasize two distinctions, which together create the four categories exhibited in Table 1:

- Does designation depend on narrow or wide context?
- Is designation "automatic" given meaning and public contextual facts, or does it depend in part on the intentions of the speaker?

I'll show which expressions fit into these categories, and then explain them:

	Narrow	Wide
Automatic	I, now*, here*	tomorrow, yea
Intentional	now, here	that, this man, there

TABLE 1 Types of indexicals

Narrow versus wide contexts.

The narrow context consists of the constitutive facts about the utterance, which I will take to be the agent, time and position. These roles are filled with every utterance. The clearest case of an indexical that relies only on the narrow context is "I", whose designation depends on the agent and nothing else.

The wider context consists of those facts, plus anything else that might be relevant, according to the workings of a particular indexical.

The sorts of factors on which an indexical can be made to depend seem, in principle, limitless. For example,

It is yea big.

means that it is as big as the space between the outstretched hands of the speaker, so this space is a contextual factor in the required sense for the indexical "yea".

Automatic versus intentional indexicals.

When Rip Van Winkle says, "I fell asleep yesterday," he intended to designate (let us suppose), July 3, 1766. He in fact designated July 2, 1786, for he awoke twenty years to the day after he fell asleep. An utterance of "yesterday" designates the day before the utterance occurs, no matter what the speaker intends. Given the meaning and context, the designation is automatic. No further intention, than that of using the words with their ordinary meaning, is relevant.

The designation of an utterance of "that man", however, is not automatic. The speaker's intention is relevant. There may be several men standing across the street when I say, "That man stole my jacket". Which of them I refer to depends on my intention.

However, we need to be careful here. Suppose there are two men across the street, Harold dressed in brown and Fred in blue. I think that Harold stole my wallet and I also think wrongly that the man dressed in blue is Harold. I intend to designate Harold *by* designating the man in blue. So I point towards the man in blue as I say "that man". In this case I designate the man in blue—even if my pointing is a bit off target. My intention to point to the man in blue is relevant to the issue of whom I designate, and what I say, but my intention to refer to Harold is not. In this case, I say something I don't intend to say, that Fred, the man in blue, stole my wallet, and fail say what I intended to, that Harold did. So it is not just any referential intention that is relevant to demonstratives, but only the more basic ones, which I will call *directing intentions*, following Kaplan 1989.

In a case like this I will typically perceive the man I refer to, and may often point to or otherwise demonstrate that person. But neither perceiving nor pointing seems necessary to referring with a demonstrative.

The indexicals "I", "now", and "here" are often given an honored place as "pure" or "essential" indexicals. Some writers emphasize the possibility of translating away other indexicals in favor of them— replacing "today" for example with "the day it is now", or "this pencil" with "the pencil to which I now attend".[3] In Table 1, this honored place is represented by the cell labeled "narrow" and "automatic". However, it is not clear that "now" and "here" deserve this status, hence the asterisks. With "here" there is the question of how large an area is to

---

[3] See, for example, Castañeda 1967, Corazza 1996.

count, and with "now" the question of how large a stretch of time. If I say, "I left my pen here," I would be taken to designate a relatively small area, say the office in which I was looking. If I say, "The evenings are cooler than you expect here" I might mean to include the whole San Francisco Bay area. In "Now that we walk upright, we have lots of back problems," "now" would seem to designate a large if indefinite period of time that includes the very instant of utterance, while in "Why did you wait until now to tell me?" it seems to designate a considerably smaller stretch. It seems then that these indexicals really have an intentional element.

4 Post-semantic Uses of Context

We contrasted presemantic and semantic uses of context. There is a third use, which I call "post-semantic". In this type of case we lack the materials we need for the proposition expressed by a statement, even though we have identified the words and their meanings, and consulted the contextual factors to which the indexical meanings direct us. Some of the constituents of the proposition expressed are *unarticulated*, and we consult the context to figure out what they are.

Compare the following pairs of sentences:

(6a) It is raining

(6b) It is raining here

(7a) They are serving drinks at the local bar

(7b) They are serving drinks at the bar near here

In many circumstances, (6a) and (6b) would convey exactly the same information, that it was raining where the speaker was. In both cases, the place where the rain must be taking place for the statement to be true is supplied by the context. But there is an important difference in how this place is supplied. In (6b) there is a part of the sentence, the indexical 'here', that designates the place. The relevant contextual fact is simply the place of the utterance. In (6a) there is no item in the sentence that designates the place. The contextual fact that provides the place is simply that it is obvious to everyone that the speaker is talking about the weather in the place she is at.

Suppose the speaker is talking on the phone with a relative who lives a number of miles away, where there has been a drought. She interrupts the conversation to utter (6a) to her family, gathered near the phone. In this case the reference is to the place where the relative is, not to the place where the speaker is. It is simply the facts about the speaker's intentions, perhaps limited by what the speaker can expect the audience to figure out, that determines which place is being talked about when (6a) is used.

In this case, I say that the place is an *unarticulated constituent* of the proposition expressed by the utterance. It is a constituent, because, since rain occurs at a time in a place, there is no truth-evaluable proposition unless a place is supplied. It is unarticulated, because there is no morpheme that designates that place.[4]

The words 'local' in (7a) and 'near' in (7b) both identify a relation between objects (like bars) and locations. They different syntactically, in that 'local' has one argument place, for the bar, while 'near' has two, one for the bar and one for the location. But a location is needed with 'local ' too; to determine whether (7a) is true or not, we need to determine not only which bars are serving drinks, but relative to which location the crucial bar is local. In many cases it will be the location where the speaker is, but it need not be. As a continuation of the aside mentioned above, (7a) could be a remark about the location where the relative on the other end of the phone finds himself, deciding whether to be dry or get wet.

I call the case of unarticulated constituents "post-semantic". The task of identifying the unarticulated constituents of the propositions expressed by an utterance remains after all of the relevant semantic rules have been understood and applied.

Return for a moment to (6a) and (6b).

(6a) It is raining.

(6b) It is raining here.

Here are two cases. Case 1: Fred hears Mary say (6a); he doesn't know whether she is talking about the location where they are, or some other location—perhaps the location of the person to whom she is talking

---

[4]Calling this phenomenon "unarticulated constituents" instead of, say, "implicit reference" is simply meant to focus on what I think as the starting point of investigation, the question of how there can be a constituent in the proposition, with no corresponding expression in the utterance. I sometimes use more common and traditional term "implicit reference" for what the speaker does, that leads to there being a constituent that is unarticulated. But I think the term "implicit reference" is sometimes thought to be necessarily connected to what I regard as special case. In some cases of implicit reference there is a feature, a trace, a sort of phantom expression, that serves in place of an expression, so the referred to constituent really isn't unarticulated. Linguists often agree on the criteria for and presence of such features; it is a robust phenomenon. But I do think that saying there is such a feature should amount to more than saying that we use an $n - 1$-place predicate for an n-ary relation. I am interested in the theoretical possibility and coherence of truly unarticulated constituents; I also hope, however, that I have found some convincing examples that they really occur.

on the phone. So, in a sense, he doesn't know what she has said. Case 2; Fred reads a postcard Mary has written (6b). He doesn't know where she was when she sent it, so, in a sense, he doesn't know what she said.

In Case 1, Fred has a task to perform once he understands the meaning of the sentence he hears. He has to figure out what location Mary was talking about. In performing this task, the semantics of the words of (6a) do not provide a guide. Fred will be guided, in figuring out what location Mary is talking about, by his knowledge of the particular situation. Who is Mary talking to? What is she likely to be trying to say? And so forth.

In Case 2, once Fred understands the meaning of the sentence he reads, he has also task to perform, in order to understand what was said. Again, he needs to know what location Mary was talking about. But here semantics provides a partial guide. He needs to identify the location she was at to serve as the designation of the use of "here". Because he knows the meaning of "here," Fred knows exactly what fact is relevant. He doesn't need to know much about Mary; just where she is and that she is using English.

5 Unarticulated Constituents: When Things are Not Worth Mentioning

Now I want to make some points about the conditions under which we leave the constituents of what we say unarticulated. I am not offering anything like a comprehensive account, only making some observations. Of course, the general theme is clear: we don't articulate the objects we are talking about, when it is obvious what they are from the context.

The first type of case are those in which, with respect to a certain n-ary relationship, there is a unique object that always plays a certain argument role for a certain population. Perhaps the residents of Z-land never get any information about the weather any where else, and don't care anyway. When they say, "It is raining," they mean, "It is raining in Z-land". They use a $n - 1$-place predicate to convey information about an n-ary relation. Here are four more examples of this sort of case:

- A population (children, say) who only get information about what time it is in their own time zone, and only take actions whose success depends on things happening at particular times in their own time zone. They report the time with the 1-place predicate, "It's ( ) o'clock". But the relation they are conveying information about it is a 2-ary relation: *It's n o'clock at place p.*

- An agent that never needs to have information about how the world looks except from its own perspective. It will treat n-ary relations involving itself as $n-1$ ary relations, and treat properties of itself as propositions, for example, *Bird in front!* rather than *Bird in front of me.*

- If we think of our own world as just one of many possible worlds (David Lewis style), then each contingent relation has an argument place for the world. But our language ignores this. The actual world is an unarticulated constituent of our thought and speech.

- According to physics, every judgment about time is true only relative to an inertial frame; "simultaneous" is a 3-ary relation; but we normally treat it as a 2-ary relation, ignoring the inertial frame parameter.

In these examples I have not carefully distinguished between constituents that are unarticulated in speech and those that are not even thought of. In Perry 1986 I try to develop some helpful vocabulary for making this distinction.

In the second kind of case I want to discuss, the occupant of the unarticulated argument role does not stay the same, as in all of the examples of the first kind of case. Although the occupant changes, the relation of the occupant to the agent is always the same.

Suppose the Z-landers use the 1-place predicate "Rains(t)" for the 2-ary relation of rain at a place at a time. But they have become nomads. The place at issue (the one that determines the truth of their utterances and the success of the actions based on them) is the place they are at, at the time of the utterance.

Note that, unlike the originals Z-landers, these folks will get in trouble if they try to accumulate information about raining: It didn't rain 2 days ago, it didn't rain yesterday, it didn't rain today, so it won't rain tomorrow.

Cases of the third type are like those of the first type except that properties of the entire set of objects that occupy the unarticulated parameter have been noticed and incorporated into the language. If we adopt the Lewis perspective on possible worlds, then our concepts of necessity and possibility are like this. I don't articulate the possible world I am at, and I don't talk about how things are at other specific worlds. But I recognize in addition to properties of the possible world I am at properties of the set of worlds. "Philosophy is necessarily fascinating," for example, is true if philosophy is fascinating in all of the possible worlds.

6 Concluding Remarks

Let us say that we talk about an object, when we express propositions that have that object as a constituent. We have a variety of ways of talking about objects, including referring to them indexically, describing them, naming them, and as we have seen, not mentioning them explicitly at all. At a first pass, we might say that indexicals provide a way of talking about objects that doesn't require us to know much about what they are like or what their names are, but does require that we know what relation they have to us—or more accurately, to the context of utterance. Descriptions and names provide ways of talking about objects that don't require us or our listeners to know the relations of those object to us, but do require us to know what they are like or what they are named.

For example, I can refer to Bill Clinton as "you" if I am talking to him. I don't need to know his name or much about him. A more likley case is that I refer to him by name or describe him, while I have no idea of whether he is in Washington or Los Angeles or abroad—and thus have no ability to even point in his general direction, refer to him demonstratively.

Implicit reference is appropriate when it is obvious who or what is being spoken about, for one reason or another. But the reasons for this obviousness can be quite varied. In one kind of case, the constituent may be left unarticulated because it is so centrally involved in the agent's concept of the relation in question, that he has never really separated the constituent from the relation. In another, all that is special about the object is that right at that point in the conversation, it just is obvious that it is the one that would be talked about.

References

Almog, Joseph, John Perry and Howard Wettstein, eds. 1989. *Themes From Kaplan*. New York: Oxford University Press.

Castañeda, Hector-Neri. 1966. "He": A Study in the Logic of Self-Consciousness. *Ratio* 8, 130–57.

Castañeda, Hector-Neri. 1967. Indicators and Quasi-Indicators. *American Philosophical Quarterly* 4, 85–100.

Condoravdi, Cleo and Mark Gawron. 1996. The Context Dependency of Implicit Arguments. In Makoto Kanazawa, Christopher Piñón, and Henriëtte de Swart, eds., *Quantifiers, Deduction and Context*, 1–32. CSLI Lecture Notes. Stanford: CSLI.

Corazza, Eros. 1996. *Reference, Contexte et Attitudes*. Paris-Montreal: Vrin-Bellarmin.

Kaplan, David. 1989. Demonstratives. In Almog, Joseph, John Perry and Howard Wettstein, eds., *Themes From Kaplan*, 481–563. New York: Oxford University Press.

Partee, Barbara. 1989. Binding Implicit Variables in Quantified Contexts. *Papers of the Chicago Linguistic Society* 25, 342–365.

Perry, John. 1986. Thought Without Representation. *Supplementary Proceedings of the Aristotelian Society*, Vol. 60, 263–283. Reprinted in (Perry 1993, 205–218).

Perry, John. 1993. *The Problem of the Essential Indexical and Other Essays*. New York: Oxford University Press.

Perry, John. 1997. Indexicals and Demonstratives. In Robert Hale and Crispin Wright, eds., *Companion to the Philosophy of Language*. Oxford: Blackwells.

Perry, John. 1997. Reflexivity, Indexicality and Names. in Wolfang Künne, Albert Newen, and Martin Anduschus (eds)., *Direct Reference, Indexicality, and Propositional Attitudes*. Stanford, CA: CSLI Publications.

Perry, John. 1997. Rip Van Winkle and Other Characters. In *The European Journal of Analytical Philosophy*. Forthcoming.

2

Formalizing Context (Expanded Notes)

JOHN MCCARTHY AND SAŠA BUVAČ

These notes discuss formalizing contexts as *first class objects*. The basic relations are

$ist(c, p)$ meaning that the proposition p is true in the context c, and

$value(c, e)$ designating the value of the term e in the context c.

Besides these there are *lifting formulas* that relate the propositions and terms in subcontexts to possibly more general propositions and terms in the outer context. Subcontexts are often specialized with regard to time, place and terminology.

Introducing contexts as formal objects will permit axiomatizations in limited contexts to be expanded to *transcend* the original limitations. This seems necessary to provide AI programs using logic with certain capabilities that human fact representation and human reasoning possess. Fully implementing transcendence seems to require further extensions to mathematical logic, i.e. beyond the nonmonotonic inference methods first invented in AI and now studied as a new domain of logic.

Our papers are available to WWW browsers at http://www-formal.stanford.edu. The development of these ideas has benefitted from discussions with Johan van Benthem, Tom Costello, Richard Fikes, Mike Genesereth, Fausto Giunchiglia, R. V. Guha, Ian Mason, and Carolyn Talcott. Guha wrote his thesis Guha 1991 while this article was going through many versions as the ideas developed, and the mutual influences cannot be specified. This work was partly supported by DARPA contract NAG2-703 and ARPA/ONR grant N00014-94-1-0775.

Computing Natural Language.
Atocha Aliseda, Rob van Glabbeek, and Dag Westerståhl, editors.

1 Introduction

These notes contain some of the reasoning behind the proposals of Mc-Carthy 1987 to introduce contexts as formal objects. The present proposals are incomplete and tentative. In particular the formulas are not what we will eventually want, and we will feel free to use formulas in discussions of different applications that aren't always compatible with each other. This is an expanded and revised version of McCarthy 1993. An earlier version of this paper is the Stanford University Technical Note STAN-CS-TN-94-13. The current version contains new sections §7 and §13, as well as updated bibliographical remarks. Some of the results in this paper have been previously also published in one of the following: Buvač and McCarthy 1996, Buvač 1996a, Buvač 1996b.

Our object is to introduce contexts as abstract mathematical entities with properties useful in artificial intelligence. Our attitude is therefore a computer science or engineering attitude. If one takes a psychological or philosophical attitude, one can examine the phenomenon of contextual dependence of an utterance or a belief. However, it seems to us unlikely that this study will result in a unique conclusion about *what context is*. Instead, as is usual in AI, various notions will be found useful.

One major AI goal of this formalization is to allow simple axioms for common sense phenomena, e.g. axioms for static blocks world situations, to be *lifted* to contexts involving fewer assumptions, e.g. to contexts in which situations change. This is necessary if the axioms are to be included in general common sense databases that can be used by any programs needing to know about the phenomenon covered but which may be concerned with other matters as well. Rules for lifting are described in section 4 and an example is given.

A second goal is to treat the context associated with a particular circumstance, e.g. the context of a conversation in which terms have particular meanings that they wouldn't have in the language in general.

The most ambitious goal is to make AI systems which are never permanently stuck with the concepts they use at a given time because they can always *transcend* the context they are in—if they are smart enough or are told how to do so. To this end, formulas $ist(c, p)$ are always considered as themselves asserted within a context, i.e. we have something like $ist(c', ist(c, p))$. The regress is infinite, but we will show that it is harmless.

The main formulas are sentences of the form

$$c' : \quad ist(c, p),$$

which are to be taken as assertions that the proposition p is true in the context c, itself asserted in an outer context c'. (We have adopted

Guha's Guha 1991 notation rather than that of McCarthy 1987, because he built his into Cyc, and it was easy for us to change ours.) For now, propositions may be identified with sentences in English or in various logical languages, but we may later take them in the sense of McCarthy 1979b as abstractions with possibly different identity conditions. We will use both logical sentences and English sentences in the examples, according to whichever is more convenient.

Contexts are abstract objects. We don't offer a definition, but we will offer some examples. Some contexts will be *rich* objects, like situations in situation calculus. For example, the context associated with a conversation is rich; we cannot list all the common assumptions of the participants. Thus we don't purport to describe such contexts completely; we only say something about them. On the other hand, the contexts associated with certain microtheories are poor and can be completely described.

Here are some examples.

$c0$: $ist(context\text{-}of(\text{"Sherlock Holmes stories"}),$

"Holmes is a detective")

asserts that it is true in the context of the Sherlock Holmes stories that Holmes is a detective. We use English quotations here, because the formal notation is still undecided. Here $c0$ is considered to be an *outer context*. In the context $context\text{-}of(\text{"Sherlock Holmes stories"})$, Holmes's mother's maiden name does not have a value. We also have

$c0$: $ist(context\text{-}of(\text{"U.S. legal history"}),$

"Holmes is a Supreme Court Justice").

Since the outer context is taken to be the same as above, we will omit it in subsequent formulas until it becomes relevant again. In this context, Holmes's mother's maiden name has a value, namely Jackson, and it would still have that value even if no-one today knew it.

$ist(c1, at(jmc, Stanford))$ is the assertion that John McCarthy is at Stanford University in a context in which it is given that jmc stands for the first author of this paper and that *Stanford* stands for Stanford University. The context $c1$ may be one in which the symbol at is taken in the sense of being regularly at a place, rather than meaning momentarily at the place. In another context $c2$, $at(jmc, Stanford)$ may mean physical presence at Stanford at a certain instant. Programs based on the theory should use the appropriate meaning automatically.

Besides the sentence $ist(c, p)$, we also want the term $value(c, term)$ where *term* is a term. For example, we may need $value(c, time)$, when c is a context that has a time, e.g. a context usable for making assertions about a particular situation. The interpretation of $value(c, term)$ involves a problem that doesn't arise with $ist(c, p)$. Namely, the space in which terms take values may itself be context dependent. However, many applications will not require this generality and will allow the domain of terms to be regarded as fixed.

Here's another example of the value of a term depending on context:

$c0$: $value(context\text{-}of(\text{"Sherlock Holmes stories"})$,

"number of Holmes's wives") $= 0$

whereas

$c0$: $value(context\text{-}of(\text{"U.S. legal history"})$,

"number of Holmes's wives") $= 1$.

We can consider $setof\text{-}wives(Holmes)$ as a term for which the set of possible values depends on context. In the case of the Supreme Court justice, the set consists of real women, whereas in the Sherlock Holmes case, it consists of fictitious women.

The remainder of this paper is organized as follows. In §2 we give examples of some elementary relations among contexts. The basic operations of contextual reasoning, entering and exiting contexts, are introduced in §3. In §4 we focus on *lifting axioms*—axioms relating what is true in one context based on what is true in another context. Building on the basic notions of entering/exiting contexts and lifting axioms, §5 shows how contexts can be used to reason in the style of natural deduction. To illustrate short term applicability of contexts, §6 demonstrates how the context formalism aids in the integration of databases which were not originally intended to be used together. These techniques are not specific to databases and can be applied in integrating other objects, such as plans; see §7. In §8 we treat contexts associated with particular circumstances, namely those that come up in a conversation. The transcending of the outer context of a system, as is discussed in §9, might result in AI programs which are never permanently stuck with the concepts they use at a particular time. In §10, we argue that all sentences will always be context dependent, and thus it is not possible to define an absolute outermost context. Returning to applications, in §11 we sketch how contexts can be used to represent mental states and revise the beliefs of an agent. We conclude with a some remarks and conclusions in §12 and §13.

2 Relations among Contexts

There are many useful relations among contexts and also context valued functions. Here are some.

1. *specialize-time*(t, c) is a context related to c in which the time is specialized to have the value t. We may have the relation

$$c0 : \quad ist(\textit{specialize-time}(t, c), at(jmc, Stanford)) \equiv$$
$$ist(c, \textit{at-time}(t, at(jmc, Stanford))).$$

Here *at-time*(t, p) is the assertion that the proposition p holds at time t. We call this a *lifting* relation. It may be convenient to write *at-time*$(t, foo(x, y, z))$ rather than $foo(x, y, z, t)$, because this lets us drop t in certain contexts. Many expressions are also better represented using modifiers expressed by functions rather than by using predicates and functions with many arguments. Actions give immediate examples, e.g. *slowly*(*on-foot*(*go*)) rather than *go*(*on-foot,slowly*).

Instead of using the function *specialize-time*, it may be convenient to use a predicate *specializes-time* and an axiom

$$c0 : \quad \textit{specializes-time}(t, c1, c2) \wedge ist(c1, p) \supset ist(c2, \textit{at-time}(t, p)).$$

This would permit different contexts $c1$ all of which specialize $c2$ to a particular time.

There are also relations concerned with specializing places and with specializing speakers and hearers. Such relations permit lifting sentences containing pronouns to contexts not presuming specific places and persons.

2. If q is a proposition and c is a context, then *assuming*(p, c) is another context like c in which p is assumed, where "assumed" is taken in the natural deduction sense. We investigate this further in §5.

3. There is a general relation *specializes* between contexts. We say *specializes*$(c1, c2)$ when $c2$ involves no more assumptions than $c1$. We have nonmonotonic relations

$$\textit{specializes}(c1, c2) \wedge \neg ab1(p, c1, c2) \wedge ist(c1, p) \supset ist(c2, p),$$

and

$$\textit{specializes}(c1, c2) \wedge \neg ab2(p, c1, c2) \wedge ist(c2, p) \supset ist(c1, p).$$

This gives nonmonotonic inheritance of *ist* both from the subcontext to the supercontext and vice versa. More useful is the case when the sentences must change when lifted. Then we need to state that and every *proposition* meaningful in $c1$ is translatable into one meaningful in $c2$. See §4 for an example.

4. A major set of relations that need to be expressed are those between the context of a particular conversation and a subsequent written report about the situation in which the conversation took place. References to persons and objects are *decontextualized* in the report, and sentences like those given above can be used to express their relations.

5. Consider a wire with a signal on it which may have the value 0 or 1. We can associate a context with this wire that depends on time. Call it $c_{wire117}(t)$. Suppose at time 331, the value of this signal is 0. We can write this

$$ist(c_{wire117}(331), signal = 0).$$

Suppose the meaning of the signal is that the door of the microwave oven is open or closed according to whether the signal on $wire117$ is 0 or 1. We can then write the lifting relation

$$(\forall\ t)(ist(c_{wire117}(t), signal = 0) \equiv door\text{-}open(t).$$

The idea is that we can introduce contexts associated with particular parts of a circuit or other system, each with its special language, and lift sentences from this context to sentences meaningful for the system as a whole.

3   Entering and Exiting Contexts

Suppose we have the formula $c0\ :\ ist(c, p)$. We can then *enter* the context c and infer the formula $c\ :\ p$. Conversely, if we have the formula $c\ :\ p$ we can infer $c0\ :\ ist(c, p)$ by *exiting* the context c. We don't always want to be explicit about the sequence of all the contexts that were entered, but the logic needs to be such that the system always exits into the context it was in before entering. The enter and exit operations can be thought of as the push and pop operations on a stack. In the logic presented in Buvač et al. 1995 the sequence of contexts that has been entered is always explicitly stated.

We can regard $ist(c, p)$ as analogous to $c \supset p$, and the operation of entering c as analogous to *assuming* c in a system of *natural deduction* as invented by Gentzen and described in many logic texts. Indeed a context is a generalization of a collection of assumptions, but there are important differences. For example, contexts contain linguistic *assumptions* as well as declarative and a context may correspond to an infinite and only partially known collection of assumptions. Moreover, because relations among contexts are expressed as sentences in the language, $ist(c, p)$ allows inferences within the language that could only be done at the meta-level of the usual natural deduction systems.

There are various ways of handling the reasoning step of entering a context. The way most analogous to the usual natural deduction systems is to have an operation *enter c*. Having done this, one could then write any p for which one already had $ist(c, p)$. However, it seems more convenient in an interactive theorem proving to use the style of Jussi Ketonen's EKL interactive theorem prover Ketonen and Weening 1984. In the style of that system, if one had $ist(c, p)$, one could immediately write p, and the system would keep track of the dependence on c. To avoid ambiguity as to where an occurrence of $ist(\ , p)$ came from, one might have to refer to a line number in the derivation. Having obtained p by entering c and then inferring some sentence q, one can *leave c* and get $ist(c, q)$. In natural deduction, this would be called discharging the assumption c.

Human natural language risks ambiguity by not always specifying such assumptions, relying on the hearer or reader to guess what contexts makes sense. The hearer employs a *principle of charity* and chooses an interpretation that assumes the speaker is making sense. In AI usage we probably don't usually want computers to make assertions that depend on principles of charity for their interpretation.

We are presently doubtful that the reasoning we will want our programs to do on their own will correspond closely to using an interactive theorem prover. Therefore, it isn't clear whether the above ideas for implementing entering and leaving contexts will be what we want.

Sentences of the form $ist(c, p)$ can themselves be true in contexts, e.g. we can have $ist(c0, ist(c1, p))$. In this draft, we will ignore the fact that if we want to stay in first order logic, we should reify assertions and write something like $ist(c0, Ist(c1, p))$, where $Ist(c, p)$ is a term rather than a wff. Actually the same problem arises for p itself; the occurrence of p in $ist(c, p)$ might have to be syntactically distinct from the occurrence of p standing by itself. Alternatively to reifying assertions we could use a modal logic; this approach is investigated in Shoham 1991, Buvač 1996a, Amati and Pirri 1997, van Benthem 1997.

4 Lifting Axioms

Lifting axioms are axioms which relate the truth in one context to the truth in another context. Lifting is the process of inferring what is true in one context based on what is true in another context by the means of lifting axioms. We treat lifting as an informal notion in the sense that we never introduce a lifting operator. In this section we give an example of lifting. See Buvač and Fikes 1995 for more examples.

Consider a context *above-theory*, which expresses a static theory of the blocks world predicates *on* and *above*. In reasoning about the predicates themselves it is convenient not to make them depend on situations or on a time parameter. However, we need to *lift* the results of *above-theory* to outer contexts that do involve situations or times.

To describe *above-theory*, we may write informally

(1)   *above-theory* : $(\forall xy)(on(x,y) \supset above(x,y))$

(2)   *above-theory* : $(\forall xyz)(above(x,y) \wedge above(y,z) \supset above(x,z))$

etc.

which stands for

(3) $c0$: $ist(above\text{-}theory, (\forall xy)(on(x,y) \supset above(x,y)))$

etc.

Constant $c0$ denotes an outer context. Section §9 has more about $c0$. In the following formulas, we put the context in which the formula is true to the left followed by a colon.

We want to use the *above-theory* in a context *blocks* which contains the theory of blocks world expressed using situation calculus. (We assume that situations are a disjoint sort, and that the variable s ranges over the situation sort.) In the context *blocks* predicates *on* and *above* have a third argument denoting a situation. Thus the context *blocks* needs to relate its three-argument predicates $on(x,y,s)$ and $above(x,y,s)$ to two-argument predicates $on(x,y)$ and $above(x,y)$ of the *above-theory* context. This is done by introducing a context of a particular situation, *spec-sit(s)*. A context *spec-sit(s)* is associated with each situation s, such that

(4)   *blocks* : $(\forall xys)(on(x,y,s) \equiv ist(spec\text{-}sit(s), on(x,y)))$,

(5)   *blocks* : $(\forall xys)(above(x,y,s) \equiv ist(spec\text{-}sit(s), above(x,y)))$,

etc.

In order to get relations between $on(x,y,s)$ and $above(x,y,s)$, we will now import *above-theory* into the *blocks* context. The importation of *above-theory* is expressed by the axiom

(6) $c0$: $(\forall p)ist(above\text{-}theory, p) \supset ist(blocks, (\forall s)(ist(spec\text{-}sit(s), p)))$,

asserting that the facts of *above-theory* all hold in the contexts associated with every situation. The following relation between $on(x,y,s)$ and $above(x,y,s)$ follows from the above axioms.

Theorem (above):

$blocks:$ $(\forall sxy)(on(x, y, s) \supset above(x, y, s)).$

The example given is so small that it would be simpler to give the relations among the three-argument predicates directly, but imagine that *above-theory* was much larger than is given here.

We proceed to derive the above theorem.

Proof (above): We begin by assuming

(7) $blocks:$ $on(x, y, s),$

asserting that block x is on block y in a specific situation s. Together with the universally instantiated form of the $\Rightarrow$ direction of formula 4 we get

(8) $blocks:$ $ist(spec\text{-}sit(s), on(x, y)).$

Now we enter $spec\text{-}sit(s)$ and get

(9) $spec\text{-}sit(s):$ $on(x, y).$

From (3) and (6) we conclude

(10) $c0:$ $ist(blocks, (\forall s)ist(spec\text{-}sit(s), (\forall xy)on(x, y) \supset above(x, y))).$

Therefore, by entering *blocks* we have

(11) $blocks:$ $(\forall s)ist(spec\text{-}sit(s), (\forall xy)on(x, y) \supset above(x, y)).$

By universal instantiation it follows that

(12) $blocks:$ $ist(spec\text{-}sit(s), (\forall xy)on(x, y) \supset above(x, y)).$

Entering $spec\text{-}sit(s)$ gives

(13) $spec\text{-}sit(s):$ $(\forall xy)on(x, y) \supset above(x, y).$

By logic, formulas 9 and 13 give

(14) $spec\text{-}sit(s):$ $above(x, y).$

We can now either continue reasoning in $spec\text{-}sit(s)$ or exit $spec\text{-}sit(s)$ and get

(15) $blocks:$ $ist(spec\text{-}sit(s), above(x, y)).$

Together with the universally instantiated form of the $\Leftarrow$ direction of formula 5 we get

(16) $blocks:$ $above(x, y, s).$

By the deduction theorem we can discharge the initial assumption to obtain

(17) $blocks:$ $on(x, y, s) \supset above(x, y, s).$

Finally, by universal generalization it follows that

(18) *blocks* : $(\forall sxy)on(x, y, s) \supset above(x, y, s)$.

$\Box$**above**

In this derivation we used a function giving a context *spec-sit*(s) which depends on the situation parameter s. Contexts depending on parameters will surely present problems requiring more study.

Besides that, the careful reader of the derivation will wonder what system of logic permits the manipulations involved, especially the substitution of sentences for variables followed by the immediate use of the results of the substitution. There are various systems that can be used, e.g. quasi-quotation as used in the Lisp or KIF, use of back-quotes, or the ideas of McCarthy 1979b. Furthermore, the drafts of this paper have motivated a number of researchers to develop logics of context, in which (some version of) the above argument would be a derivation; these include Giunchiglia 1993, Nayak 1994, Buvač 1996a, Attardi and Simi 1998. However, at present we are more attached to the derivation than to any specific logical system.

As a further example, consider rules for lifting statements like those of section 1 to one in which we can express statements about Justice Holmes's opinion of the Sherlock Holmes stories.

5 Natural Deduction via Context

The formal theory of context can be used to represent inference and reason in the style of natural deduction. This requires lifting axioms (or lifting rules) to treat the context which a reasoning system is in as a formal object. If p is a sentence and we are in some context c, we define a new context *assuming*(c, p) so that it validates the following rules:

importation $c : p \supset q \;\vdash\; assuming(c, p) : q$
discharge $assuming(c, p) : q \;\vdash\; c : p \supset q$

Note that these rules can be replaced by lifting axioms. Thus **importation** is replaced by

(19) $(\forall cpq)(ist(c, p \supset q) \supset ist(assuming(c, p), q))$

To make the presentation simpler we write them in the rule form. An interesting rule which can be derived from the above is

assumption $\vdash\; assuming(c, p) : p$

In analogy to the restriction to the rule of $\forall$ introduction in formal systems of natural deduction, we will have to restrict the rule of universal generalization to ensure that the variable being generalized does not occur free in any of the *assuming*(c, p) terms of the current context; see Prawitz 1965.

To illustrate the rules we now give a natural-deduction style proof of the **above** theorem, which was introduced in §4. This theorem involves the lifting of the theory of above into the context of situation calculus. The proof should be compared to the Hilbert style proof which was given in §4.

Proof (above):   We begin with the $\Rightarrow$ direction of formula 4

(20) *blocks* : $(\forall xys)(on(x, y, s) \supset ist(spec\text{-}sit(s), on(x, y)))$

It follows by universal instantiation that

(21) *blocks* : $on(x, y, s) \supset ist(spec\text{-}sit(s), on(x, y))$

By the **importation** rule we get

(22) *assuming*$(blocks, on(x, y, s))$: $ist(spec\text{-}sit(s), on(x, y))$

Therefore, by entering the *spec-sit*(s) context we get

(23) *spec-sit*(s) : $on(x, y)$

Now, from formulas 3 and 6 it follows that

(24) $c0$: $ist(blocks, (\forall s)ist(spec\text{-}sit(s), (\forall xy)(on(x, y) \supset above(x, y))))$

By entering *blocks* we get

(25) *blocks* : $(\forall s)ist(spec\text{-}sit(s), (\forall xy)(on(x, y) \supset above(x, y)))$

By instantiating the universal quantifier over situations we get

(26) *blocks* : $ist(spec\text{-}sit(s), (\forall xy)(on(x, y) \supset above(x, y)))$

Therefore, by propositional logic we have

(27) *blocks* : $on(x, y, s) \supset ist(spec\text{-}sit(s), (\forall xy)(on(x, y) \supset above(x, y)))$

Therefore, by the **importation** rule we get

(28) *assuming*$(blocks, on(x, y, s))$: $ist(spec\text{-}sit(s),$
$\qquad (\forall xy)(on(x, y) \supset above(x, y)))$

Now, by entering the *spec-sit*(s) context we get

(29) *spec-sit*(s) : $(\forall xy)(on(x, y) \supset above(x, y))$

By logic from formulas 23 and 29 it follows that

(30) *spec-sit*(s) : $above(x, y)$

By exiting the *spec-sit*(s) context we get

(31) *assuming*$(blocks, on(x, y, s))$: $ist(spec\text{-}sit(s), above(x, y))$

The $\Leftarrow$ direction of formula 5

(32) $blocks:$ $(\forall xys)ist(spec\text{-}sit(s), above(x,y)) \supset above(x,y,s)$

By propositional logic we have

(33) $blocks:$ $on(x,y,s) \supset$

$\qquad\qquad (\forall xys)ist(spec\text{-}sit(s), above(x,y)) \supset above(x,y,s)$

Together with the **importation** rule the above formula allows us to infer

(34) $assuming(blocks, on(x,y,s)):$

$\qquad\qquad (\forall sxy)ist(spec\text{-}sit(s), above(x,y)) \supset above(x,y,s)$

By logic from (31) and (34) we get

(35) $assuming(blocks, on(x,y,s)):$ $above(x,y,s)$

Using the rule **discharge** it follows that

(36) $blocks:$ $on(x,y,s) \supset above(x,y,s)$

Therefore, by universal generalization we obtain what was to be proved

(37) $blocks:$ $(\forall sxy)on(x,y,s) \supset above(x,y,s)$

$\square$**above**

In the above proof we have entered the context $assuming(c,p)$ in a number of instances. This creates an interesting example because it might not be obvious in which context the term $assuming(c,p)$ is to be interpreted. However, since the logic needs to keep track of which contexts were entered in the process of reasoning, the answer becomes obvious: the term $assuming(c,p)$ will be interpreted in the next outer context (see §3 for discussion on sequences of contexts).

We gave two treatments of the key argument: one in natural deduction (§4) and one Hilbert-style (above). This kind of proof transformation is logical routine, and any textbook on proof theory (say, the recent Troelstra and Schwichtenberg 1996), tells all about it.

5.1   Postponing Preconditions via *assuming*

We conclude by noting that the *assuming* function, as defined in this section, is also useful for formalizing a number of other phenomena. Examine a naive formalism for reasoning about action where the preconditions for flying are given by the formula

(38) $c:$ $have\text{-}ticket(x) \wedge clothed(x) \supset can\text{-}fly(x).$

In common sense reasoning we want the ability to *postpone* dealing with the precondition of being clothed. This can be done by considering a context which assumes that one is clothed $assuming(c, clothed(x))$. By the **importation** rule and the formula 38 we get

(39) $assuming(c, clothed(x)) :$ $\quad have\text{-}ticket(x) \supset can\text{-}fly(x)$.

Thus in the context $assuming(c, clothed(x))$ we do not need to consider the precondition of being clothed in order to infer that one can fly.

Note that we are only developing an ontology for representing this phenomena, and are not dealing with pragmatic issues like which context a reasoning system will start in, and how the system will decide to consider a context making an additional assumption. In fact, from a pragmatic viewpoint the above process might need to be completely reversed. The reasoning system may realize that its current problem solving context c is making a particular assumption p that needs to be discharged. Then it will need to consider a context c' such that $c = assuming(c', p)$.

The *assuming* function is also needed for representing discourse. In §8 we show how it is used to handle replies to a query; in that section we call the *assuming* function *"reply"*.

See §7.2 for related examples in the planning domain.

6   Integrating Databases

We see the use of formalized contexts as one of the essential tools for reaching human level intelligence by logic based methods. However, formalized contexts have shorter term applications. In this section we deal with one short term application: we show how two data bases, which were not originally intended to be used together, can be integrated by lifting their contents into a wider context. We proceed with an example. For more practical issues involved in the task of integrating data and knowledge bases see Collet et al. 1991, Farquhar et al. 1995.

6.1   The GE, Navy, and Air Force Example

Here's a hypothetical example. Imagine that the Navy, the Air Force and General Electric have separately developed standards for databases containing facts about prices of jet engines and parts. But these standards are not the same. Suppose that associated with each item is a price. Suppose further

1. For GE, the price is a retail price not including spare parts.

2. For the Navy, the price is the Government's purchase price including spare parts.

3. For the Air Force, the price includes additional inventory costs. It includes spare parts but a different assortment than the Navy's.

Now suppose that associated with each database are many programs that use the information. For example, General Electric can compute the cost of equipment packages taking into account discounts. The Navy can compute the economic ordering quantity for use when supplies get low.

Suppose now that some plan requires that unexpectedly a certain item made by General Electric is required in large quantity by both the Navy and the Air Force and deliveries and purchases from various General Electric warehouses have to be scheduled in co-ordination. The context in which the reasoning is done requires the *lifting* of various information from the contexts of the separate databases to the reasoning context. In the course of this lifting, the sentences representing the information are translated into new forms appropriate for the reasoning context.

6.2   A Simple Formalization

In this simple case, assume that the Air Force and Navy data bases need to be updated on the new General Electric prices. The GE database lists the list price, i.e. the price at which GE is selling the engine. The Navy database lists the price which Navy *will need to pay* for the engine and its assortment of spare parts, if it decides to use GE.

In order to reason with multiple databases, c_{ps}, an ad hoc context for reasoning about the particular problem, may be required. The problem solving context c_{ps} contains objects denoting the General Electric context c_{GE}, the Navy context c_N, and the Air Force context c_{AF}. This enables us to talk about facts which are contained in the corresponding databases. If for example the GE database contains a fact $price(FX\text{-}22\text{-}engine) = \$3600K$ then the sentence

$$ist(c_{GE}, price(FX\text{-}22\text{-}engine) = \$3600K)$$

is true in c_{ps}.

Different data bases might make different assumptions. For instance, prices of engines in some contexts might or might not include spare parts or warranties. We need the ability to represent this information in c_{ps}. Function *spares*, when given a product and a context, returns the spares which the given context assumes necessary and thus includes in the price of the product. For example, $spares(c_{NAVY}, x)$ is the set of spares that Navy assumes will be included in the price of the product x. Function *warranty*, when given a product and a context, returns the name of the warranty assumed for the product in the given context. For example, $warranty(c_{NAVY}, x)$ is the name of the warranty which Navy assumes is included in the price of the product x. In this note we are treating warranty in the same manner as we would treat spare parts or additional optional features. It would be the responsibility of another formalization to "understand" the warranty and give axioms describing the exact obligations that GE has to its clients. Note that information about spares and warranties assumed by the Navy will probably not be contained in the Navy data base. (Otherwise, we would use $value(c_{\text{NAVY}}, spares(x))$ rather than $spares(c_{\text{NAVY}}, x)$ to refer to the spares that Navy assumes will be included in the price of the product x.) Rather, this information is kept in in some manual. But for these data bases to be used jointly, the spares information needs to be included; we assume that it is described declaratively in c_{ps}. Finally, the vocabulary of c_{ps} also has a function $GE\text{-}price$, which to every object assigns its corresponding price in dollars.

In the problem solving context c_{ps} we also represent the fact that GE lists engine prices without any spares, while Navy assumes spare parts to be included in the price of a product. This is done by lifting axioms, which define how the notion of price in different databases translates into the problem solving context:

(40) c_{ps} : $(\forall x)value(c_{\text{GE}}, price(x)) = GE\text{-}price(x)$

(41) c_{ps} : $(\forall x)value(c_{\text{NAVY}}, price(x)) = GE\text{-}price(x)+$

$\qquad GE\text{-}price(spares(c_{\text{NAVY}}, x))+$

$\qquad GE\text{-}price(warranty(c_{\text{NAVY}}, x))$

expressing that the price listed in the Navy data base is the price of the engine, some bag of spares, and the particular warranty that are assumed by the Navy.

(42) c_{ps} : $(\forall x)value(c_{\text{AF}}, price(x)) = f(x, GE\text{-}price(x),$

$\qquad GE\text{-}price(spares(c_{\text{AF}}, x)), GE\text{-}price(warranty(c_{\text{AF}}, x)))$

where f is some function which determines the total price of an item and spares, also taking into account the inventory cost. Note that f might not be precisely known, in which case we might decide to only give some approximate bounds on f.

Now we work out an example. Assume that we are given the prices as listed in the GE data base; i.e. the following formulas hold in c_{GE}:

(43) c_{GE} : $price(FX\text{-}22\text{-}engine) = \$3600K$

(44) c_{GE} : $price(FX\text{-}22\text{-}engine\text{-}fan\text{-}blades) = \$5K$

(45) c_{GE} : $price(FX\text{-}22\text{-}engine\text{-}two\text{-}year\text{-}warranty) = \$6K$

Information about spares and warranties will not be found in the c_{GE} data base and will probably require looking up in some manual or description of the the data base. We need to enter this information into the the problem solving context:

(46) c_{ps} : $spares(c_{\mathrm{NAVY}}, \mathit{FX\text{-}22\text{-}engine}) = \mathit{FX\text{-}22\text{-}engine\text{-}fan\text{-}blades}$

(47) c_{ps} : $warranty(c_{\mathrm{NAVY}}, \mathit{FX\text{-}22\text{-}engine}) =$
$\mathit{FX\text{-}22\text{-}engine\text{-}two\text{-}year\text{-}warranty}$

Then we can compute the price of the FX-22 jet engine for the Navy. The following formula is a theorem, i.e. it follows from the above axioms.

Theorem (engine price):

c_{NAVY} : $price(\mathit{FX\text{-}22\text{-}engine}) = \$3611K$

In order to compute this price for the Air Force, the inventory cost given by function f would need to be known.

Proof (engine price):   First we exit the c_{GE} context thus rewriting formulas 43, 44, and 45 as

(48) c_{ps} : $value(c_{\mathrm{GE}}, price(\mathit{FX\text{-}22\text{-}engine})) = \$3600K$

(49) c_{ps} : $value(c_{\mathrm{GE}}, price(\mathit{FX\text{-}22\text{-}engine\text{-}fan\text{-}blades})) = \$5K$

(50) c_{ps} : $value(c_{\mathrm{GE}}, price(\mathit{FX\text{-}22\text{-}engine\text{-}two\text{-}year\text{-}warranty})) = \$6K$

From formulas 40 and 48 it follows that

(51) c_{ps} : $\mathit{GE\text{-}price}(\mathit{FX\text{-}22\text{-}engine}) = \$3600K$

From formulas 40 and 49 it follows that

(52) c_{ps} : $\mathit{GE\text{-}price}(\mathit{FX\text{-}22\text{-}engine\text{-}fan\text{-}blades}) = \$5K$

Therefore, using formula 46, we get

(53) c_{ps} : $\mathit{GE\text{-}price}(spares(c_{\mathrm{NAVY}}, \mathit{FX\text{-}22\text{-}engine})) = \$5K$

In a similar fashion, from formulas 40, 47 and 50 we can conclude that

(54) c_{ps} : $\mathit{GE\text{-}price}(warranty(c_{\mathrm{NAVY}}, \mathit{FX\text{-}22\text{-}engine})) = \$6K$

From formulas 51, 53, and 54 if follows that

(55) c_{ps} : $\mathit{GE\text{-}price}(\mathit{FX\text{-}22\text{-}engine})+$
$\mathit{GE\text{-}price}(spares(c_{\mathrm{NAVY}}, \mathit{FX\text{-}22\text{-}engine}))+$
$\mathit{GE\text{-}price}(warranty(c_{\mathrm{NAVY}}, x)) = \$3611K$

Then, using formula 41 we can conclude that

(56) c_{ps} : $value(c_{\mathrm{NAVY}}, price(\mathit{FX\text{-}22\text{-}engine})) = \$3611K$

By entering c_{NAVY} we get

(57) $\quad c_{\text{NAVY}} : \quad price(\textit{FX-22-engine}) = \$3611K$

$\Box$**engine–price**

In the above proof we are assuming that all constants denote the same object in all contexts, i.e. that all constants are *rigid designators*. Consequently constants can be substituted for universally quantified variables by the universal instantiation rule. Generalizing the proof is straight forward if we drop this assumption.

6.3 Formalization for Bargaining

Now assume that the air force database contains the price air force *plans to pay* for a product, i.e. the price *included in the budget*. Like before, the GE database contain the list price, which will probably be higher than the air force budget price. This formalization is suited for use by some bargaining agents or programs. The bargaining agent for the air force will through negotiation attempt to convince the GE agent to lower the GE list price to the air force budget price (or some price that would be acceptable to the air force).

The bargaining agents will work in some problem solving context c_{ps}. This context contains constants denoting the various data bases which will be relevant to the bargaining; in our case these will be the General Electric context c_{GE}, and the Air Force context c_{AF}. Context c_{ps} contains functions which represent the budget price and the list price of a product. Function *manufacturer-price*, when given a context of a manufacturer and a product, returns the price at which the product is offered for sale by the manufacturer; functions *budget-price*, when given a context of a customer and a product, returns the price which the customer is willing to pay for the product. Like in the previous example, c_{ps} can represent the spares associated with an engine. Function *spares*, when given a product and an object, returns the spares which the given context assumes necessary and thus included in the price of the product.

The air force and GE will need to bargain in order to negotiate a price which is acceptable to both parties. However, since unlike GE, the air force assumes that the price will include a set of spare parts, the lifting axioms will be needed to adjust the prices in the two data bases to ensure that both the budget price and the list price pertain to the same package. The lifting axioms are:

(58) $\quad c_{\text{ps}} : (\forall x)\, value(c_{\text{GE}}, price(x)) = \textit{manufacturer-price}(c_{\text{GE}}, x)$

(59) $\quad c_{\text{ps}} : (\forall x)\, value(c_{\text{AF}}, price(x)) = \textit{budget-price}(c_{\text{AF}}, x)+$

$$budget\text{-}price(c_{\mathrm{AF}}, spares(c_{\mathrm{AF}}, x))$$

The lifting axioms will enable us to derive the *budget-price* and *manufacturer-price* prices in c_{ps}, both of which pertain to the engine only, excluding any spares. These can then be used by the bargaining programs to negotiate a price and administrate a sale.

Note again the difference between this formalization and the previous one. In the previous subsection the *price* function in both data bases referred to the price which was actually being paid for a product. Therefore, the lifting axioms were used to directly infer the price in one data base based on the price listed in another. In this example, on the other hand, given the list price the lifting axioms can not be used to work out the budget price. The lifting axioms simply ensure that both the list price and the budget price talk only about the engine, and do not implicitly assume the inclusion of spare parts.

6.4 Treating *value* as an Abbreviation

It will be possible to define *value* as an abbreviation in a modal context language which contains the *ist*. (Such reductions might be problematic in non-modal approaches, such as Attardi and Simi 1998.)

We first deal with the case where all contexts have the same domains. We define *value* as an abbreviation:

(60) $\quad value(c, x) = y \quad \equiv \quad (\forall z) y = z \equiv ist(c, x = z)$

Eliminating the *value* abbreviation, the above formulas are equivalent to:

(61) $\quad c_{\mathrm{ps}} : \quad (\forall xy) ist(c_{\mathrm{GE}}, y = price(x)) \equiv y = GE\text{-}price(x)$

(62) $\quad c_{\mathrm{ps}} : \quad (\forall xy) ist(c_{\mathrm{NAVY}}, y = price(x)) \equiv y = GE\text{-}price(x) +$
$$GE\text{-}price(spares(c_{\mathrm{NAVY}}, x))$$

(63) $\quad c_{\mathrm{ps}} : \quad (\forall xy) ist(c_{\mathrm{AF}}, y = price(x)) \equiv$
$$y = f(x, GE\text{-}price(x), GE\text{-}price(spares(c_{\mathrm{AF}}, x)))$$

6.5 Existence as a Predicate

Not all objects will typically exist in all contexts. To deal with this phenomena, we introduce existence as a predicate, $E(c, x)$. Intuitively,

$$E(c, x)$$

is true iff the object denoted by x exists in the context denoted by c.

If the domains of all the contexts are not the same, then formulas 60—63 are not intuitively correct. Instead, a domain precondition needs to be added to all the formulas. For example instead of formula 61, we would write

$$(64) \quad c_{\text{ps}}: \quad (\forall xy)(E(c,x) \wedge E(c,y)) \supset$$
$$(ist(c_{\text{GE}}, y = price(x))) \equiv y = GE\text{-}price(x))$$

The main implication connective in this formula might not be classical (see Buvač et al. 1995).

Note however, if we simply change the abbreviation of *value* to

$$(65) \quad value(c,x) = y \quad \equiv \quad E(c,x) \supset (\forall z)(E(c,z) \supset$$
$$(y = z \equiv ist(c, x = z)))$$

then the axioms involving *value* (axioms 40-42 and 58-59) will still be true. In other words, the previous domain formalizations remain unaltered. To verify this, note that substituting this new definition for value (given in formula 65) into formula 40 gives us formula 64, rather then formula 61.

We also need to assert that the problem solving context c_{ps} contains all the objects present in the other contexts which are involved in the particular problem solving process. In some outer context $c0$ we would write:

$$(66) \quad c0: \quad (\forall c)involved\text{-}in\text{-}ps(c) \supset (\forall x)(E(c,x) \supset E(c_{\text{ps}},x)).$$

In both cases mentioned above, the rules of entering and exiting a context for the *value* function will follow from the general rules enter and exit for the *ist*.

This approach is similar to the treatment of existence in quantificational modal logics which are based on free logics; see Thomason 1970. Many of the philosophical issues involved in quantifying across worlds with different domains apply also here; see Kripke 1971 for discussion. For example, it is well known from quantificational modal logic that the classical rule of universal instantiation is not valid for non-rigid terms. Logics of context which allow functions, will thus need to have a restricted form of universal instantiation.

7 Combining Planning Contexts

Integrating plans, which were not originally designed to be used together, is a task that frequently comes up in real world applications. However, this task is typically performed by humans. Contexts enable us to formalize this style of reasoning, thus providing a logical basis for developing computer programs which will be able to mechanically integrate plans produced by different systems.

The main contribution of this section is showing that the techniques we have used for combining data bases or knowledge bases (§4–§6) can be directly applied in combining of plans produced by different planners using different languages.

See any AI textbook, say Rich and Knight 1991, Russell and Norvig 1995 or the forthcoming Nilsson 1998, for a description of the planning problem.

7.1 Combining Planning Languages

The basic idea is to represent each subplan as though it was developed in a context. These contexts will differ, either slightly or greatly. The terminology within each subcontext is likely to be specialized, and making the plans work together requires some generalization. For this purpose we use lifting formulas, i.e. formulas that relate the propositions and terms in subcontexts to propositions and terms in an outer context.

Here is an example. Assume that a route planner, like the route optimization program of the TRAINS project Allen et al. 1995, and a supply planner, like the transportation scheduler developed at Kestrel Smith et al. 1995, have been developed independently by different groups. Given a source and a destination, the route planner will find the best route between these places. It however, has no notion of which supplies need to be transported and no notion of time. The supply planner keeps track of the supplies of some economic system and informs us which supplies need to be moved at any given time. We assume that the supply planner has no knowledge about the routes that the supplies need to travel to reach their destination.

To fill in a work order we need to integrate the information produced by the supply planner with that of the route planner. Assume that the supply planner produces

(67) *supply_planner* :   *transport*(*equipment1*,

   Rome, 11/6/95, *Frankfurt*, 1/20/96)

informing us that equipment1 needs to be transported from Rome Air Force base in New York on 11/6/95, to Frankfurt on 1/20/96. The context constant *supply_planner* denotes the context in which supply planner operates and reports its results. Now assume that the route planner tells us that the best route from Rome to Frankfurt is via New York City (NYC). This is represented in the context of the route planner, *route_planner*, by stating

(68) *route_planner* :   [*Rome, NYC, Frankfurt*] =

   route(*Rome, Frankfurt*).

Note that *route* is a function returning a list which encodes the best route. Integrating this information inside the problem solving context, *ps*, we get

(69) *ps* :   *transport(equipment1, [Rome, NYC, Frankfurt],*

$\qquad$ 11/6/95, 1/20/96)

stating that equipment1 needs to be transported by the route Rome–NYC–Frankfurt departing on 11/6/95 and arriving on 1/20/96. This information can now be entered into the work order. Note that the same predicate symbol, *transport*, is used in different ways in two different contexts: its arity and its arguments are different in the *supply_planner* context and in the *ps* context.

The context formalism enables us to capture this style of reasoning in logic. We write *lifting axioms* which describe how the information from different contexts can be integrated. In the above example the lifting formula is

(70) *ps* : $(\forall x)(\forall l1)(\forall l2)(\forall d1)(\forall d2)$

$\qquad$ *ist(supply_planner, transport(x, l1, d1, l2, d2))* $\supset$

$\qquad$ *transport(x, value(route_planner, route(l1, l2)), d1, d2).*

If the formula *transport(x, l1, d1, l2, d2)* is true in the context of the supply planner, then the formula

$\qquad$ *transport(x, value(route_planner, route(l1, l2)), d1, d2)*

holds in the problem solving context. Intuitively, formula 70 expresses that if the supply planner states that some items x need to be transported leaving $l1$ on $d1$ and arriving to $l2$ on $d2$, and if

$\qquad$ *value(route_planner, route(l1, l2))*

is reported by the route planner as the best route from $l1$ to $l2$, then the information which can be entered into the work order is

$\qquad$ *transport(x, value(route_planner, route(l1, l2)), d1, d2).*

In other words, formula 70 specifies the integrating of a plan which involves the notions of time and supplies produced by the supply planner with the details involving a route produced the route planner. The lifting axiom 70 allows us to derive the plan given by formula 69 in the problem solving context *ps* from the plans given by formulas 67 and 68 in the contexts of their corresponding planners.

A term with a definite meaning in one context often needs translation when used in another context. Thus *Rome* may mean Rome NY in a data base of US Air Force bases but needs translation when a formula is lifted to a context of worldwide geography. Lifting formulas similar to 70 can be used to do this type of translation.

7.2 Discharging Kindness Assumptions

Any plan produced from the lifting axiom 70 makes numerous assumptions. For example, it assumes that the shortest path will always get the cargo to its destination on time. Although this assumption is usually valid, we can imagine a scenario in which an urgent delivery will need to take a longer route in order to get to its destination on time. We thus need to consider the timeliness of a path in scenarios which involve urgent deliveries.

In robotics, assumptions of this sort are commonly called *kindness assumptions*, cf. Nourbakhsh and Genesereth 1996, because they amount to assuming that the world is kind, i.e. that things will turn out in our favor most of the time. Kindness assumptions are a useful tool and are commonly made both when constructing and integrating plans. They allow us to focus on the aspects of a plan that seem to be relevant to the problem at hand and to disregard details which we assume will hold for that particular problem class. However, whenever kindness assumptions are made it is important to have a mechanism which enables us to discharge such assumptions and reason about their validity in cases when it is unclear whether they hold. The context formalisms enables us to do this in the framework of logic.

Assume that after deriving the plan in formula 69 (by integrating the plans from the route and supply planning contexts) we realize that the delivery is needed urgently. At this point our goal is to discharge the timeliness assumption and take the proposed path through NYC only if it gets equipment1 to Frankfurt on time. The desired plan, which is given in an urgent problem solving context *ps_urgent*, is thus

(71) $ps\_urgent:$ $timely\_route(11/6/95, 1/20/96,$

$\qquad [Rome, NYC, Frankfurt])) \supset transport(equipment1,$

$\qquad [Rome, NYC, Frankfurt], 11/6/95, 1/20/96)$

where deciding whether *timely_route* holds will involve looking up airplane schedules and local delivery facilities in some data base. We are assuming that conditional plans, like formula 71, can be represented by the system. In the general case, formula 71 follows from formula 69 and the lifting axiom

(72) $ps\_urgent:$ $(\forall x)(\forall r)(\forall d1)(\forall d2)ist(ps, transport(x, r, d1, d2)) \supset$

$\qquad timely\_route(d1, d2, r) \supset transport(x, r, d1, d2).$

In some planning instances we will want to consider the timeliness issues at the very outset. We can avoid using the original problem solving context *ps* by inferring a lifting theorem which integrates a plan from the route planner and a plan from the supply planner to directly produce a plan in *ps_urgent*

(73) *ps_urgent* : $(\forall x)(\forall r)(\forall l1)(\forall l2)(\forall d1)(\forall d2)$

$(ist(supply\_planner, transport(x, l1, l2, d1, d2))\wedge$

$timely\_route(d1, d2, value(route\_planner, route(l1, l2)))) \supset$

$transport(x, value(route\_planner, route(l1, l2)), d1, d2)$

Formula 73 logically follows from the lifting axioms given in formula 70 and formula 72.

7.3 Combining Heterogeneous Objects

It is often necessary to combine objects that were not designed to work together. These objects may be databases of facts, programs, hardware or plans. Even if the objects were intended to be used together, maintenance of adherence to their specifications and ensuring the consistency of terminology through time is often difficult. Each object was developed in a context, and these contexts differ, either slightly or greatly. The terminology within each subcontext is likely to be specialized, and making them work together requires some generalization.

We have described an approach based on our formal theory of context.

8 Representing Discourse

In this section we illustrate context change by showing how our formalism can be used to represent the context of a conversation in which terms have particular meanings that they wouldn't have in the language in general. The analysis that follows is along the lines of van Benthem 1996.

We examine question/answer conversations which are simply sequence of questions and answers. In this simple model we allow two types of questions:

propositional questions are used to inquire whether a proposition is true or false; they require a yes or no answer. In the language we introduce a special proposition *yes* which is used to answer these questions.

qualitative questions are used to find the objects of which a formula holds; in the language we introduce a unary predicate *answer* which holds of these objects.

In order to know what is being communicated in a discourse, as well as reason about a discourse in general, we need a way of representing the discourse. To do this in the framework of the formal theory of context, we identify a new class of contexts, the *discourse contexts*. Discourse contexts are not only characterized by the sentences which are true in them but also by the intended meaning of their predicates, which might vary from one discourse context to the next.

We represent a discourse with a sequence of discourse contexts, each of which in turn represents the discourse state after an utterance in the discourse. Our attention is focused only on discourses which are sequences of questions and replies: $[q^1, r^1, q^2, r^2, \ldots, q^n, r^n]$. Thus, we can represent such a discourse with a sequence of discourse contexts:

$$[c_d, query(c_d, q^1), reply(query(c_d, q^1), r^1), \ldots$$

$$\ldots, reply(query(reply(\cdots reply(query(c_d, q^1), r^1) \cdots, r^{n-1}), q^n), r^n)]$$

s.t. (i) $c_d{}^0$ is some discourse context in which the initial question (q^1) was asked; (ii) the function *query* takes a question ϕ and some discourse context c_d (representing the discourse state before the question ϕ) and returns the discourse context representing the discourse state after asking the question ϕ in c_d; (iii) the function *reply* takes a reply ϕ and some discourse context c_d (representing the discourse state before before replying ϕ) and returns the discourse context representing the discourse state after replying ϕ in c_d. In order to reason about the discourse we now only need the properties of the functions *query* and *reply*. These will be made precise in the next subsection. Similar representation of discourse in logic is often used by linguists; eg. Stalnaker 1998, Beaver 1997.

Since we are not concerned with solving the syntactic and semantic problems addressed by the natural language community, we are assuming the system is given the discourse utterances in the form of logical formulas. This assumption is in line with McCarthy 1990a; in McCarthy's terminology we would say that the discourse has been processed by both the parser and the understander to produce a logical theory. Note that the process of producing this theory is not precisely defined, and it is not completely clear how much common sense information is needed to generate it. It might turn out that producing such a theory requires the solution of the problem we had set out to solve. But for the time being let us take a positive perspective and assume the discourse theory is given; for further discussion of this point see Israel 1990, Kameyama 1994, Thomason 1997, Buvač 1997. Note that our simple model does not claim to capture all aspects of discourse interpretation. We have refrained from modeling some phenomena that have been studied by semanticists and computational linguists. In particular, Discourse Representation Theory, Kamp 1981, includes a third aspect of discourse interpretation, namely discourse entities known as *reference markers*. Reference markers, each of which can be accessible at a given point in a discourse, are now viewed as an essential element of most theories of context that deal with anaphoric reference. Furthermore, we have ignored pragmatic aspects relevant to discourse analysis; see Grosz and Sidner 1986. These include resolving references by keeping track of which objects are salient in a discourse, and inferring the intentions of agents based on their speech acts.

8.1 The Logic of *query* and *reply*

In this section we give the properties of the functions *query* and *reply*, which are central for representing question/answer discourses. Since the *query* and *reply* functions are treated in the style of situation calculus, we do not need to change our basic theory of context, but simply give the axioms that formalize the two functions.

Intuitively, the *query* function will set up a context in which the reply to the question will be interpreted. For example, the context resulting in asking some proposition p will have the property that *yes* in that context will be interpreted as p. Thus *query* only changes the semantic state of the discourse context. The *reply* function will do a simple update of information: the formulas true in the context resulting in replying p in c_d will be exactly those formulas which are conditionally true on p in c_d. Thus the *reply* function only changes the epistemic state of the discourse context. We now make these notions more precise.

The following axioms characterize the functions *query* and *reply*.

interpretation axiom (propositional) if ϕ is a closed formula, then

$$ist(query(c, \phi), \phi \equiv yes)$$

frame axiom (propositional) if ϕ is a closed formula, and *yes* does not occur in ψ, then

$$ist(c, \psi) \supset ist(query(c, \phi), \psi)$$

interpretation axiom (qualitative) if x is the only variable occurring free in ϕ, then

$$ist(query(c, \phi(x)), \phi(x) \equiv answer(x))$$

frame axiom (qualitative) if x is the only variable occurring free in ϕ, and *answer* does not occur in ψ, then

$$ist(c, \psi) \supset ist(query(c, \phi(x)), \psi)$$

reply axiom $\quad ist(reply(c, \phi), \psi) \equiv ist(c, \phi \supset \psi)$

The predicate $answer(x)$ is used to return an answer to a qualitative question, similar to the way it is commonly used to return a witness in a resolution theorem prover; see Green 1969.

We proceed to illustrate the axioms and their use with an example.

8.2 Example: Air Force–GE Discourse

We examine the following hypothetical discourse taking place between the Air Force and General Electric:

1. AF: Will you bid on the engine for the FX22?
2. GE: Yes.
3. AF: What is your bid?
4. GE: $4M.
5. AF: Does that include spares?
6. GE: Yes.

We transcribe the above discourse in our logic as a sequence of discourse contexts, s.t.

$c1 = query(c, \textit{will-bid-on}(engine(\text{FX22})))$
$c2 = reply(c1, yes)$
$c3 = query(c2, price(engine(\text{FX22}), x))$
$c4 = reply(c3, answer(\$4M))$
$c5 = query(c4, price(x) \equiv ist(c_{\text{kb}}, \textit{price-including-spares}))$
$c6 = reply(c5, yes)$

where c is the initial discourse context. To simplify presentation, in this section we take *price* to be a predicate; in §4 we have illustrated how it can be treated as a function by using *value* instead of *ist*.

8.3 Deriving Properties of the Air Force–GE Discourse

We now show some properties of the discourse which can be derived with our logic.

8.3.1 First Question: Propositional Case

The discourse begins with a propositional question. We show how they modify the discourse state.

Theorem ($c2$): $ist(c2, \textit{will-bid-on}(engine(\text{FX22})))$

Proof ($c2$): Instantiating the first axiom for the propositional questions, we get

$$ist(query(c, \textit{will-bid-on}(engine(\text{FX22}))),$$
$$\textit{will-bid-on}(engine(\text{FX22})) \equiv yes)$$

which, by definition of $c1$, can be written as

$$ist(c1, \textit{will-bid-on}(\textit{engine}(\text{FX22})) \equiv \textit{yes})$$

Instantiating the axiom for reply we have

$$ist(\textit{reply}(c1, \textit{yes}), \textit{will-bid-on}(\textit{engine}(\text{FX22}))) \equiv$$
$$ist(c1, \textit{yes} \supset \textit{will-bid-on}(\textit{engine}(\text{FX22})))$$

and it follows from the two lines above that

$$ist(\textit{reply}(c1, \textit{yes}), \textit{will-bid-on}(\textit{engine}(\text{FX22})))$$

which by definition of $c2$ we can write as

$$ist(c2, \textit{will-bid-on}(\textit{engine}(\text{FX22})))$$

$\square_{\mathbf{c2}}$

8.3.2   Second Question: Qualitative Case

The reasoning for this qualitative question is similar to the propositional question.

Theorem $(c4)$: $ist(c4, \textit{price}(\textit{engine}(\text{FX22}), \$4M))$

Proof $(c4)$:   We begin with an instance of the first axiom for qualitative questions

$$ist(\textit{query}(c2, \textit{price}(\textit{engine}(\text{FX22}), x)),$$
$$\textit{price}(\textit{engine}(\text{FX22}), x) \equiv \textit{answer}(x))$$

which, by definition of $c3$, can be written as

$$ist(c3, \textit{price}(\textit{engine}(\text{FX22}), x) \equiv \textit{answer}(x))$$

Instantiating the axiom for reply we have

$$ist(\textit{reply}(c3, \textit{answer}(\$4M)), \textit{price}(\textit{engine}(\text{FX22}), \$4M)) \equiv$$
$$ist(c3, \textit{answer}(\$4M) \supset \textit{price}(\textit{engine}(\text{FX22}), \$4M))$$

and it follows from the two lines above that

$$ist(\textit{reply}(c3, \textit{answer}(\$4M)), \textit{price}(\textit{engine}(\text{FX22}), \$4M))$$

which by definition of $c4$ we can write as

$$ist(c4, \textit{price}(\textit{engine}(\text{FX22}), \$4M))$$

$\square_{\mathbf{c4}}$

Due to the frame axioms, the conclusion established in the first question

$$ist(c2, \textit{will-bid-on}(\textit{engine}(\text{FX22})))$$

also holds in context $c4$.

Theorem (frame): $ist(c2, will\text{-}bid\text{-}on(engine(\text{FX22})))$

Proof (frame):   We first instantiate the second axiom for qualitative questions to get

$ist(c2, will\text{-}bid\text{-}on(engine(\text{FX22}))) \supset$

$ist(query(c2, price(engine(\text{FX22}), x)), will\text{-}bid\text{-}on(engine(\text{FX22})))$

The two lines above imply

$ist(query(c2, price(engine(\text{FX22}), x)), will\text{-}bid\text{-}on(engine(\text{FX22})))$

which, by definition of $c3$, can be written as

$ist(c3, will\text{-}bid\text{-}on(engine(\text{FX22})))$

Now we apply the following instance of the reply axiom

$ist(reply(c3, answer(\$4M)), will\text{-}bid\text{-}on(engine(\text{FX22}))) \equiv$

$ist(c3, answer(\$4M) \supset will\text{-}bid\text{-}on(engine(\text{FX22})))$

to get

$ist(reply(c3, answer(\$4M)), will\text{-}bid\text{-}on(engine(\text{FX22})))$

which, by definition of $c4$, can be written as

$ist(c4, will\text{-}bid\text{-}on(engine(\text{FX22})))$

$\square$**frame**

8.3.3   Third Question: Dealing with Ambiguity

We are assuming that the predicate *price* is ambiguous in the discourse contexts since it can be ambiguously interpreted as either the predicate *price-including-spares* or as the predicate *price-not-including-spares* in some knowledge base. In the third question the predicate is disambiguated for context $c6$. This will allow us to prove that the GE bid on the FX22 engine is \$4M including spare parts. Note that we will have to state the above in the kb context because the discourse contexts are not expressive enough to distinguish between the price including spares and the price excluding spares (which in fact was the source of ambiguity).

Theorem (kb): $ist(c_{\text{kb}}, price\text{-}including\text{-}spares(engine(\text{FX22}), \$4M))$

Proof (kb):   By reasoning similar to the first question, we can conclude

$ist(c6, price(x, y)) \equiv ist(c_{\text{kb}}, price\text{-}including\text{-}spares(x, y))$

From the frame axioms we get

$ist(c6, price(engine(\text{FX22}), \$4M))$

similarly to the frame derivation in the second question. Now the theorem follows from the above formulas. $\square_{\mathbf{kb}}$
See Buvač 1996b for more details.

9 Transcending Contexts

Human intelligence involves an ability that no-one has yet undertaken to put in computer programs—namely the ability to *transcend* the context of one's beliefs.

That objects fall would be expected to be as thoroughly built into human mental structure as any belief could be. Nevertheless, long before space travel became possible, the possibility of weightlessness was contemplated. It wasn't easy, and Jules Verne got it wrong when he thought that there would be a turn-over point on the way to the moon when the travelers, who had been experiencing a pull towards the earth would suddenly experience a pull towards the moon.

In fact, this ability is required for something less than full intelligence. We need it to be able to comprehend someone else's discovery even if we can't make the discovery ourselves. To use the terminology of McCarthy and Hayes 1969, it is needed for the *epistemological* part of intelligence, leaving aside the heuristic.

We want to regard the system as being at any time within an implicit outer context; we have used $c0$ in this paper. Thus a sentence p that the program believes without qualification is regarded as equivalent to $ist(c0, p)$, and the program can therefore infer $ist(c0, p)$ from p, thus *transcending* the context $c0$. Performing this operation again should give us a new outer context, call it c_{-1}. This process can be continued indefinitely. We might even consider continuing the process transfinitely, for example, in order to have sentences that refer to the process of successive transcendence. However, I have no present use for that.

However, if the only mechanism we had is the one described in the previous paragraph, transcendence would be pointless. The new sentences would just be more elaborate versions of the old. The point of transcendence arises when we want the transcending context to relax or change some assumptions of the old. For example, our language of adjacency of physical objects may implicitly assume a gravitational field, e.g. by having relations of *on* and *above*. We may not have encapsulated these relations in a context. One use of transcendence is to permit relaxing such implicit assumptions.

The formalism might be further extended to provide so that in c_{-1} the whole set of sentences true in c_0 is an object $truths(c0)$.

Transcendence in this formalism is an approach to formalizing something that is done in science and philosophy whenever it is necessary to go from a language that makes certain assumptions to one that does not. It also provides a way of formalizing some of the human ability to make assertions about one's own thoughts.

The usefulness of transcendence will depend on there being a suitable collection of nonmonotonic rules for *lifting* sentences to the higher level contexts.

As long as we stay within a fixed outer context, it seems that our logic could remain ordinary first order logic. Transcending the outermost context seems to require a changed logic with what Tarski and Montague call *reflexion principles*. They use them for sentences like $true(p*) \equiv p$, e.g " 'Snow is white.' is true if and only if snow is white."

The above discussion concerns the epistemology of transcending contexts. The heuristics of transcendence, i.e. when a system should transcend its outer context and how, is entirely an open subject.

10   Relative Decontextualization

Quine [1969] uses a notion of "eternal sentence", essentially one that doesn't depend on context. This seems a doubtful idea and perhaps incompatible with some of Quine's other ideas, because there isn't any language in which eternal sentences could be expressed that doesn't involve contexts of some sort. We want to modify Quine's idea into something we can use.

The usefulness of eternal sentences comes from the fact that ordinary speech or writing involves many contexts, some of which, like pronoun reference, are valid only for parts of sentences. Consider, "Yes, John McCarthy is at Stanford University, but he's not at Stanford today". The phrase "at Stanford" is used in two senses in the same sentence. If the information is to be put (say) in a book to be read years later by people who don't know McCarthy or Stanford, then the information has to be decontextualized to the extent of replacing some of the phrases by less contextual ones.

The way we propose to do the work of "eternal sentences" is called *relative decontextualization*. The idea is that when several contexts occur in a discussion, there is a common context above all of them into which all terms and predicates can be lifted. Sentences in this context are "relatively eternal", but more thinking or adaptation to people or programs with different presuppositions may result in this context being transcended.

11 Mental States as Outer Contexts

A person's state of mind cannot be adequately regarded as the set of propositions that he believes—at least not if we regard the propositions as sentences that he would give as answers to questions. For example, as we write this we believe that George Bush is the President of the United States, and if we were entering information in a database, we might write

$$president(U.S.A.) = George.Bush.$$

However, my state of mind includes, besides the assertion itself, my reasons for believing it, e.g. he has been referred to as President in today's news, and we regard his death or incapacitation in such a short interval as improbable. The idea of a TMS (see Doyle 1979) or reason maintenance system is to keep track of the pedigrees of all the sentences in the database and keep this information in an auxiliary database, usually not in the form of sentences.

Our proposal is to use a database consisting entirely of *outer* sentences where the pedigree of an *inner* sentence is an auxiliary parameter of a kind of modal operator surrounding the sentence. Thus we might have the outer sentence

$$believe(president(U.S.A.) = George.Bush, because\ldots),$$

where the dots represent the reasons for believing that Bush is President.

The use of formalized contexts provides a convenient way of realizing this idea. In an outer context, the sentence with reasons is asserted. However, once the system has committed itself to reasoning with the proposition that Bush is President, it enters an inner context with the simpler assertion

$$president(U.S.A.) = George.Bush.$$

If the system then uses the assertion that Bush is President to reach a further conclusion, then when it leaves the inner context, this conclusion needs to acquire a suitable pedigree.

Consider a belief revision system that revises a database of beliefs solely as a function of the new belief being introduced and the old beliefs in the system. Such systems seem inadequate even to take into account the information used by TMS's to revise beliefs. However, it might turn out that such a system used on the outer beliefs might be adequate, because the consequent revision of inner beliefs would take reasons into account.

12   Remarks

1. Guha has put contexts into Cyc, largely in the form of microtheories. The *above-theory* example is a microtheory. See Guha 1991 for some of the details.

2. We have mentioned various ways of getting new contexts from old ones: by specializing the time or place, by specializing the situation, by making abbreviations, by specializing the subject matter (e.g. to U.S. legal history), by making assumptions and by specializing to the context of a conversation. These are all specializations of one kind or another. Getting a new context by transcending an old context, e.g. by dropping the assumption of a gravitational field, gives rise to a whole new class of ways of getting new contexts.

These are too many ways of getting new contexts to be treated separately.

3. We have used natural language examples in this article, although natural language is not our main concern. Nevertheless, we hope that formalizing context in the ways we propose may be useful in studying the semantics of natural language. Natural language exhibits the striking phenomenon that context may vary on a very small scale; several contexts may occur in a single sentence.

Consider the context of an operation in which the surgeon says, "Scalpel". In context, this may be equivalent to the sentence, "Please give me the number 3 scalpel".

4. $ist(c, p)$ can be considered a modal operator dependent on c applied to p. In this sense much of our analysis amounts to reasoning in a certain systems of modal logic or temporal logic; see Chellas 1980, Gabbay et al. 1993, Blackburn and de Rijke 1997.

In the propositional case, given a context language containing a set of contexts C, we can define a modal language containing modalities $\Box_1, \Box_2, \ldots$, one for each context from C. By replacing each occurrence of $ist(c_\beta, \phi)$ with $\Box_\beta \phi$, we can define a bijective translation function which to each formula of the propositional context logic assigns a well-formed modal formula. Based on this translation, Buvač et al. 1995 shows a reduction of the propositional logic of context to a propositional multimodal logic. Similar results are obtained using proof theoretic tools in Giunchiglia and Serafini 1994.

However, these results do not carry over to the quantificational case. The quantificational logic of context, for example, enables us to state that the formula ϕ is true in contexts which satisfy some property $p(x)$ as follows:$(\forall v)p(v) \supset ist(v, \phi)$. This formula has no obvious translation into standard multi-modal logic, and the meaning of such formulas which quantify over modalities is beyond the analysis commonly done in quantificational modal logic. See Buvač 1996a for details.

5. Proof theoretic approach to context has been emphasized by Richard W. Weyhrauch and Fausto Giunchiglia and his group. See Weyhrauch 1980, Weyhrauch et al. 1998, Giunchiglia 1993, Giunchiglia and Serafini 1994, Cimatti and Serafini 1995.

6. It would be useful to have a formal theory of the natural phenomenon of context, e.g.in human life, as distinct from inventing a form of context useful for AI systems using logic for representation. This is likely to be an *approximate theory* in the sense described in McCarthy 1979a. That is, the term "context" will appear in useful axioms and other sentences but will not have a definition involving "if and only if". Hayes 1997 outlines one such taxonomy of contexts.

7. Useful nonmonotonic rules for lifting will surely be more complex than the examples given. See Etherington and Crawford 1996 for context limited consistency check.

8. Theories along the lines of Barwise and Perry 1983 are in many ways similar to formal theories of context; van Benthem 1997 gives one comparison. Menzel 1996, Akman and Surav 1997 represent context using the tools of situation theory.

9. Gabbay 1996 proposes fibred semantics as a way of "weaving of logics". For a comparison of this approach to the formal theories of context, see Gabbay and Nossum 1997.

13   Conclusion

Our main motivation for formalizing contexts is to deal with the problem of generality in AI. We want to be able to make AI systems which are never permanently stuck with the concepts they use at a given time because they can always transcend the context they are in. Such a capability would allow the designer of a reasoning system to include only such phenomena as are required for the system's immediate purpose, while retaining the assurance that if a broader system is required later, "lifting axioms" can be devised to restate the facts from the narrower context to the broader one, with qualifications added as necessary. Thus, a necessary step in the direction of addressing the problem of generality in AI is providing a language which enables representing and reasoning with multiple contexts and expressing lifting axioms. In this paper we provide such a language.

The goal is that no matter what corners the specialists paint themselves into, what they do can be *lifted* out and used in a more general context.

For an overview of the AI research on formalizing context see Akman and Surav 1996. For technical papers on context in AI and Linguistics see the following special issues of journals: Perlis 1995, Iwanska and Zadrozny 1997, Buvač and Kameyama 1998.

References

Akman, Varol, and Mehmet Surav. 1996. Steps toward Formalizing Context. *AI Magazine* 17(3):55–72.

Akman, Varol, and Mehmet Surav. 1997. The use of situation theory in context modeling. *Computational Intelligence* 13(3). To appear.

Allen, James F., Lenhart K. Schubert, George Ferguson, Peter Heeman, Chung Hee Hwang, Tsuneaki Kato, Marc Light, Nathaniel G. Martin, Bradford W. Miller, Massimo Poesio, and David R. Traum. 1995. A Formalization of Viewpoints. *Journal of Experimental and Theoretical AI* 7:7–48.

Amati, Gianni, and Fiora Pirri. 1997. Contexts as relativized definitions: a formalization via fixed points. In *Context in KR & NL*. MIT, Cambridge, Mass. AAAI Fall Symposium. To appear.

Attardi, Giuseppe, and Maria Simi. 1998. Communication across Viewpoints. *Journal of Logic Language and Information*. To appear.

Barwise, Jon, and John Perry. 1983. *Situations and Attitudes*. Cambridge: MIT Press.

Beaver, David Ian. 1997. Presupposition. In *Handbook of Logic and Language*, ed. Johan van Benthem and Alice ter Meulen. Elsevier—MIT Press.

van Benthem, Johan. 1996. *Exploring Logical Dynamics*. CSLI Publications. Distributed by Cambridge University Press.

van Benthem, Johan. 1997. Changing Contexts and Shifting Assertions. In *this volume*.

Blackburn, Patrick, and Maarten de Rijke. 1997. *Specifying Syntactic Structures*. CSLI Publications. Distributed by Cambridge University Press.

Buvač, Saša. 1996a. Quantificational Logic of Context. In *Proceedings of the Thirteenth National Conference on Artificial Intelligence*.

Buvač, Saša. 1996b. Resolving lexical ambiguity using a formal theory of context. In *Semantic Ambiguity and Underspecification*, ed. Kees Van Deemter and Stanley Peters. CSLI Publications. Distributed by Cambridge University Press: CSLI Lecture Notes Number 55.

Buvač, Saša. 1997. Pragmatical Considerations on Logical AI. In *Context in KR & NL*. MIT, Cambridge, Mass. AAAI Fall Symposium. To appear.

Buvač, Saša, Vanja Buvač, and Ian A. Mason. 1995. Metamathematics of Contexts. *Fundamenta Informaticae* 23(3).

Buvač, Saša, and Richard Fikes. 1995. A Declarative Formalization of Knowledge Translation. In *Proceedings of the ACM CIKM: The 4th International Conference on Information and Knowledge Management*.

Buvač, Saša, and Megumi Kameyama. 1998. Introduction: Toward a Unified Theory of Context? *Journal of Logic Language and Information*. Special issue on Context in Linguistics and AI. To appear.

Buvač, Saša, and John McCarthy. 1996. Combining Planning Contexts. In *Advanced Planning Technology—Technological Achievements of the ARPA/Rome Laboratory Planning Initiative*, ed. Austin Tate. AAAI Press.

Chellas, Brian F. 1980. *Modal Logic, an Introduction*. Cambridge University Press.

Cimatti, A., and L. Serafini. 1995. Multi-Agent Reasoning with Belief Contexts: the Approach and a Case Study. In *Intelligent Agents: Proceedings of 1994 Workshop on Agent Theories, Architectures, and Languages*, ed. M. Wooldridge and N. R. Jennings, 71–85. Lecture Notes in Computer Science, No. 890. Springer Verlag. Also IRST-Technical Report 9312-01, IRST, Trento, Italy.

Collet, C., M. Huhns, and W. Shen. 1991. Resource Integration Using a Large Knowledge Base in Carnot. *IEEE Computer* 24(12):55–62.

Doyle, Jon. 1979. A Truth Maintenance System. *Artificial Intelligence* 12:231–272.

Etherington, David W., and James M. Crawford. 1996. Toward Efficient Default Reasoning. In *Proceedings of the Thirteenth National Conference on Artificial Intelligence*.

Farquhar, Adam, Angela Dappert, Richard Fikes, and Wanda Pratt. 1995. Integrating Information Sources using Context Logic. Technical Report KSL-95-12. Knowledge Systems Laboratory, Stanford University. Also appears in the 1995 AAAI Spring Symposium on Information Gathering from Distributed, Heterogeneous Environments.

Gabbay, D. M., C. J. Hogger, and J. A. Robinson (ed.). 1993. *Handbook of Logic in Artificial Intelligence and Logic Programming, Volume 1 and Volume 4*. Oxford University Press.

Gabbay, Dov. 1996. Fibred semantics and the weaving of logics: Part I: Modal and intuitionistic logics. *Journal of Symbolic Logic* 61(4):1057–1120.

Gabbay, Dov, and Rolf Nossum. 1997. Structured Contexts with Fibred Semantics. In *Proceedings of the International and Interdisciplinary Conference on Context*.

Giunchiglia, F. 1993. Contextual reasoning. *Epistemologia, special issue on I Linguaggi e le Macchine* XVI:345–364. Short version in Proceedings IJ-

CAI'93 Workshop on Using Knowledge in its Context, Chambery, France, 1993, pp. 39–49. Also IRST-Technical Report 9211-20, IRST, Trento, Italy.

Giunchiglia, F., and L. Serafini. 1994. Multilanguage Hierarchical Logics (or: how we can do without modal logics). *Artificial Intelligence* 65:29–70. Also IRST-Technical Report 9110-07, IRST, Trento, Italy.

Green, C. Cordell. 1969. Theorem Proving by Resolution As a Basis for Question Answering Systems. In *Machine Intelligence 4*, ed. Bernard Meltzer and Donald Michie. 183–205. Edinburgh, Scotland: Edinburgh University Press.

Grosz, Barbara J., and Candace L. Sidner. 1986. Attention, Intention, and the Structure of Discourse. *Computational Linguistics* 12:175–204.

Guha, R. V. 1991. *Contexts: A Formalization and Some Applications*. Doctoral dissertation, Stanford University. Also technical report STAN-CS-91-1399-Thesis, and MCC Technical Report Number ACT-CYC-423-91.

Hayes, Pat. 1997. The Contextual Ambiguity of "Context". In *Context in KR & NL*. MIT, Cambridge, Mass. AAAI Fall Symposium. To appear.

Israel, D. J. 1990. On Formal versus Commonsense Semantics. In *Theoretical Issues in Natural Language Processing*, ed. Y. Wilks. Hillsdale, NJ: Lawrence Erlbaum Associates.

Iwanska, Lucja, and Wlodek Zadrozny. 1997. Special issue on Context in Natural Language Processing. *Computational Intelligence* 13(3). To appear.

Kameyama, Megumi. 1994. Indefeasible semantics and defeasible pragmatics. In *Quantifiers, Deduction, and Context*, ed. Makoto Kanazawa, Christopher Pinon, and Henriette de Swart. CSLI, Stanford, CA. Also SRI International Technical Note 544 and CWI Report CS-R9441,1994.

Kamp, Hans. 1981. A Theory of Truth and Discourse Representation. In *Formal Methods in the Study of Language*, ed. J. Groenendijk, T. Janssen, and M. Stokhof. Amsterdam: Mathematical Centre Tracts 135.

Ketonen, Jussi, and Joseph S. Weening. 1984. EKL—An Interactive Proof Checker: User's Reference Manual. Technical report. Computer Science Department, Stanford University, Stanford, California.

Kripke, Saul A. 1971. Semantical Considerations on Modal Logic. In *Reference and Modality*, ed. Leonard Linsky. Oxford University Press. Oxford Readings in Philosophy.

McCarthy, John. 1979a. Ascribing mental qualities to machines. In *Philosophical Perspectives in Artificial Intelligence*, ed. Martin Ringle. Humanities Press. Reprinted in McCarthy 1990b.

McCarthy, John. 1979b. First Order Theories of Individual Concepts and Propositions. In *Machine Intelligence*, ed. Donald Michie. Edinburgh: Edinburgh University Press. Reprinted in McCarthy 1990b.

McCarthy, John. 1987. Generality in Artificial Intelligence. *Comm. of ACM* 30(12):1030–1035. Also in *ACM Turing Award Lectures, The First Twenty Years*, ACM Press, 1987; and reprinted in McCarthy 1990b.

McCarthy, John. 1990a. An Example for Natural Language Understanding and the AI Problems it Raises. In *Formalizing Common Sense: Papers by John McCarthy*. 355 Chestnut Street, Norwood, NJ 07648: Ablex Publishing Corporation.

McCarthy, John. 1990b. *Formalizing Common Sense: Papers by John McCarthy*. 355 Chestnut Street, Norwood, NJ 07648: Ablex Publishing Corporation.

McCarthy, John. 1993. Notes on Formalizing Context. In *Proceedings of the Thirteenth International Joint Conference on Artificial Intelligence*.

McCarthy, John, and Patrick Hayes. 1969. Some philosophical problems from the standpoint of artificial intelligence. In *Machine Intelligence*, ed. B. Meltzer and D. Michie. 463–502. Edinburgh: Edinburgh University Press. Reprinted in McCarthy 1990b.

Menzel, Christopher. 1996. Contexts and Information. In *The Third Symposium on Logical Formalizations of Commonsense Reasoning*. Stanford University. Preliminary report; updated versions available at http://philebus.tamu.edu/~cmenzel.

Nayak, P. Pandurang. 1994. Representing Multiple Theories. In *Proceedings of the Twelfth National Conference on Artificial Intelligence*.

Nilsson, Nils J. 1998. *Artificial Intelligence: A New Synthesis*. Morgan Kaufmann. To appear.

Nourbakhsh, Illah R., and Michael R. Genesereth. 1996. Making Assumptions to Simplify Planning. *Autonomous Robots* 1(3).

Perlis, D. 1995. Papers on Context: Theory and Practice. *Fundamenta Informaticae* 23(3).

Prawitz, Dag. 1965. *Natural Deduction: A Proof-Theoretical Study*. Stockholm, Göteborg, Uppsala: Almqvist & Wiksell Boktryckeri AB.

Rich, Elaine, and Kevin Knight. 1991. *Artificial Intelligence*. McGraw-Hill, Inc. 2 edition.

Russell, Stuart, and Peter Norvig. 1995. *Artificial Intelligence, a Modern Approach*. Prentice Hall.

Shoham, Yoav. 1991. Varieties of Context. In *Artificial Intelligence and Mathematical Theory of Computation: Papers in Honor of John McCarthy*, ed. Vladimir Lifschitz. Academic Press.

Smith, D. R., E. A. Parra, and S. J. Westfold. 1995. Synthesis of High-Performance Transportation Schedulers. Technical Report KES.U.95.1. Kestrel Institute. http://kestrel.edu/www/publications.html.

Stalnaker, Robert. 1998. On the Representation of Context. *Journal of Logic Language and Information*. To appear.

Thomason, Richmond H. 1970. Some Completeness Results for Modal Predicate Calculi. In *Philosophical Problems in Logic*, ed. Karel Lambert. D. Reidel Publishing Company/ Dordrecht-Holland. Synthese Library, Humanities Press, New York.

Thomason, Richmond H. 1997. Nonmonotonicity in Linguistics. In *Handbook of Logic and Language*, ed. Johan van Benthem and Alice ter Meulen. Elsevier—MIT Press.

Troelstra, A. S., and H. Schwichtenberg. 1996. *Basic Proof Theory*. Cambridge University Press. Cambridge Tracts in Theoretical Computer Science 43.

Weyhrauch, Richard W. 1980. Prolegomena to a Theory of Mechanized Formal Reasoning. *Artificial Intelligence* 13(1):133–176.

Weyhrauch, Richard W., Marco Cadoli, and Carolyn L. Talcott. 1998. Using Abstract Resources to Control Reasoning. *Journal of Logic Language and Information*. To appear.

3

Changing Contexts and Shifting Assertions

JOHAN VAN BENTHEM

1 Why This Note?

The motivation for this contribution are some interesting ideas recently put forward by John McCarthy and John Perry, concerning the interplay between changing contexts and shifting forms of linguistic expression accessing these. (Cf. McCarthy 1993, Perry 1993—as well as their contributions to this Volume). Although coming from a computer scientist and a philosopher with different aims, the two proposals have enough in common (at least for a logician looking from a distance) to warrant joint discussion. The editors have invited me to provide a catalyst, if not a synthesis. For this purpose, I have picked one particular theme in the work of these authors—which may be called 'logical perspective'. I will discuss mechanisms for changing contexts and shifting assertions across these. Modal and first-order languages will serve as concrete models highlighting this phenomenon. From this logical stance, some new issues of general interest emerge, too.

2 The Overloading of 'Context'

The term 'context' has a wide variety of uses in logic, linguistics, and recently also in AI. It tastes a bit like 'system', 'situation' or 'state', in that it combines broad intuitive appeal with a promise of precise structure. Nevertheless, there is such a diversity of uses of 'context' that no single notion may underlie all of them. Nor have there been evident intuitions concerning contexts that have generated anything like a 'context theory'. Philosophers often use context to stand for everything that is needed in addition to a piece of syntactic or acoustic code in order to

Computing Natural Language.
Atocha Aliseda, Rob van Glabbeek, and Dag Westerståhl, editors.
Copyright © 1998, Stanford University.

obtain a complete proposition. This mostly programmatic 'everything else' is quite diverse, with ingredients ranging from the physical state of the environment of utterance to social conventions in a language game. (Indeed, Perry's paper highlights some of this.) In linguistics, Cresswell, Kaplan and others have shown since the seventies how context gives us the changing 'perspective' from which to evaluate indexicals ("you", "there"), while Stalnaker, Gazdar, van der Sandt, and others have used contexts as states of propositional commitment to understand the discourse dynamics of presuppositions. (Zimmermann 1984 is an excellent survey.) But contexts have also been used for changing domains of quantification, reference groups for measure predicates, variable assignments for anaphora, or information states for modals or conditionals. (Cf. Muskens et al. 1997 for some of these dynamic themes.) Clearly, no single conception underlies all of this, although we may try to classify broad uses. For instance, on some accounts, information states are like informative theories about the world, while on others, they are indexical perspectives providing views of the world. In Artificial Intelligence, McCarthy's program shows a similar variety, with some intended applications making contexts look like data bases, and others more like small idealized parts of the world. McCarthy certainly writes as if the notion of context is clear, once put on the agenda, and merely needs some honest tending to blossom. Moreover, he writes as if context were an ontological kind of object, rather than a convenient methodological fiction (which is what most of the above cases exemplify). Either way, is there anything substantial to a notion that has been diluted this much? I think one can remain a sceptic about this (my own example proves it), while still acknowledging various interesting themes raised by context theorists that are well worth studying. Again, I will confine myself to logical changes in perspective.

3 The Interplay Between Assertions and Contexts

Briefly, Perry is concerned with understanding the flexibility and efficiency of mechanisms of reference in natural language as we use it, McCarthy rather with the design of efficient modular systems in artificial intelligence. These different motivations, one aiming for description, the other for design, show many analogies, which give rise to similar logical issues. For instance, both authors are concerned with the transfer of information from one context to another. The main principle driving this (in my interpretation) is one of *Minimal Representation*. Roughly speaking, in communication, we use minimal linguistic code while taking maximal advantage of structure available in the relevant context.

(Similar minimality principles have been put forward for the design of robots that must reason, and yet perform on-line: cf. Rosenschein and Kaelbling 1986, Barwise 1989.) But when changing contexts (e.g., to take someone else's point of view, or to change the subject, or to access background information), this linguistic form may be modified, too—to lift the relevant information from its original setting. Amongst others, Perry has isolated Pacific islanders discussing their weather. For their purposes, it suffices to refer to events and times—while place indicators are redundant (say, "rain now" or "sunshine yesterday"). But when the larger world comes into play, place indicators may become necessary to convey the local facts ("it is raining here, but not over there" or "it is raining at latitude X and longitude Y"). Put very simply, one may switch between local evaluation of a simple statement p in context c and global evaluation of a more complex explicitly 'context-stamped' statement $P(c)$ in a larger environment $\mathbf{M}$:

$$\mathbf{c} \models p \qquad \text{iff} \qquad \mathbf{M} \models P(c)$$

This is a two-way process, of course. Retreat into a smaller context allows us to skip indicators whose values are understood. McCarthy describes similar switches when discussing 'entering' and 'exiting' of contexts. In addition, he brings in a calculus of situations, involving *translations* relating, e.g., implicit and explicit local positions of objects x, y in situations and associated contexts:

$$\text{ON}(x, y, \mathbf{s}) \qquad \text{iff} \qquad \text{IST}(\mathbf{c_1}(\mathbf{s}), \text{on}(x, y))$$

Here, the truth predicate IST is the same as the above semantic turn-style $\models$. These moves involve operations on linguistic assertions. But McCarthy's work also suggests operations transforming contexts themselves, such as 'transcendence' (naming a current context to make it an object of discourse), 'restriction' simplifying a complex situation, or forms of 'merge' combining contexts. Similar phenomena occur in natural language, although Perry does not address these operations explicitly. Even so, both authors lack a systematic theory of *context change*, that would tell us exactly how incoming text or discourse changes a perspective or an information state. Here, one passes into the field of 'belief update and revision' and 'dynamic semantics', another currently active interface between linguistics, philosophy and AI (cf. the survey Muskens et al. 1997). So far, there has been little novel logical theory supporting the above ideas. One might say that Perry's work continues that of Kaplan, and certainly, various strands in modal and general intensional logic have developed in interaction with the latter. Likewise, McCarthy's work has inspired some logical papers of a modal slant, witness Buvač and Mason 1995, Buvač 1995. But before we turn to modal logic, let us start with basics.

4   Context Change in Standard Logic

McCarthy's and Perry's concerns unify several strands from the logical literature. First, changing arities of predicates by adding or dropping arguments is an old logical ploy. The traditional adagium for removing contradictions is to 'make a distinction'. This is often implemented by raising some k-ary predicate R in a contradictory statement $F(R)$ to a $(k+1)$-ary predicate R' with one 'hidden variable' made explicit, sorting out occurrences of R so that the new formula $F(R')$ becomes consistent. But we can say much more. In standard (first-order) logic, many technical mechanisms effect context switches with changing assertions—even when not always grouped under this heading. These may be quite diverse. Context change is not one straightforward phenomenon! Many basic results in logic relate truth of transformed formulas across transformed models. A typical example is the *Substitution Lemma*, which says that, if term t is free for x in ϕ, then

$$\mathbf{M}, a \models [t/x]\phi \quad \text{iff} \quad \mathbf{M}, a^x_{val(\mathbf{M},t,a)} \models \phi$$

Given some model $\mathbf{M}$, in environment a, one can evaluate a formula ϕ with a term t serving as an explicit instruction for computing an object ('call by name'), or equivalently, one can evaluate the bare formula ϕ in another environment $a^x_{val(\mathbf{M},t,a)}$ where the value of the term has already been computed ('call by value'). Here is another well-known example of a standard context shift, this time for domains of quantification. Making the universe of discourse explicit in syntax is the standard operation of *Relativization* . This equates evaluation of a formula ϕ in the restriction $\mathbf{M}|D$ of a first-order model $\mathbf{M}$ to some subdomain D with evaluation of the corresponding relativized formula $(\phi)^D$ in some suitable expansion $\mathbf{M}^+$ of the whole model $\mathbf{M}$:

$$\mathbf{M}|D \models \phi \qquad \text{iff} \qquad \mathbf{M}^+ \models (\phi)^{\underline{D}}$$
where $(\phi)^{\underline{D}}$ has all its quantifiers $\exists x\psi$ from ϕ relativized to
$\exists x(\underline{D}x\&\psi)$ and $\underline{D}$ is a new unary predicate denoting D in the
expanded model $\mathbf{M}^+$.

This somewhat pedantic formulation emphasizes what is really going on in this shift. A similar move drives the earlier-mentioned dynamics of domains for generalized quantifiers, whose standard ternary bounded forms $Q_E AB$ indicate obligatory shifts in the arguments E, A. Quantifier relativization is just one instance of a more general operation. This comes out in a well-known formula schema in set theory, which states the adequacy of Tarski's truth definition for models viewed as set-theoretic structures:

$$\text{for all } \mathbf{M}, \phi : \quad \mathbf{M} \models \phi \leftrightarrow (\phi)^{\underline{M}}$$

The operation on the right-hand side 'relativizes' all syntactic items interpreted by the model $\mathbf{M}$, thus displaying also the role of its interpretation function I. For instance, one specific equivalence reads as follows:

$$\mathbf{M} \models \exists x Q j x \quad \text{iff} \quad \exists x (D_{\underline{M}} x \& I_{\underline{M}}(Q)(I_{\underline{M}}(j) x)$$
adding explicit parameters for the predicate Q and for the individual constant j.

In addition to restriction, relativization and translation, there are further relevant themes in standard logic. Notably, the model theory of *preservation* deals with questions such as the following. Which first-order assertions remain true when passing from a context to a larger context? The Lós-Tarski Theorem tells us that, up to logical equivalence, these are just the purely existential formulas. This is just one example out of many (cf. Doets 1996 for a modern introduction to preservation results). We conclude that standard logic contains many results that fall under our main theme, relating shifting assertions across different models. (Of course, these are not usually grouped together in this way.) That this is a truly general phenomenon also shows in the fact that most of the above results do not depend on any particular logical formalism. The substitution and relativization lemmas hold quite generally, across first-order, second-order and other logical languages.

5 Modal Logic as a Theory of Context

As noted before, most special 'context logics' have an intensional flavour. For instance, Buvač and Mason 1995 proposes simple modal logics addressing changing perspectives. Richer modal logics of context usually do not go under this heading. But properly viewed, time and provides a good example of richer intuitions, with different grain levels showing a number of concrete interrelations. Montanari 1996 considers reductions between temporal statements in contexts of hours, days, weeks, etc.—while allowing combined information from different contexts. Indeed, the development of temporal logic over the past decades is in fact the theory of one concrete context structure. For instance, the above move bringing context explicitly into the assertion is called 'time-stamping'. Moreover, modal logics of contexts are like Prior-style tense logics, and earlier debates about the appropriateness of such modal operator formalisms vis-a-vis full first-order languages of temporal context (cf. Needham 1975) are still quite to the point. Let us now turn to further specifics. Technically, McCarthy's and Perry's examples are reminiscent of modal *Correspondence* Theory (van Benthem 1984), which translates modal assertions into first-order ones over the same Kripke models, making reference to and quantification over worlds (or any kind of intensional indices, including contexts) fully explicit. Thus, for propositional modal logic, we have correspondences like the following (with α an assignment setting the linguistic context variable c to the real context $\mathbf{c}$):

$$\mathbf{M}, \mathbf{c} \models p \quad \text{iff} \quad \mathbf{M}, \alpha \models Pc$$
$$\mathbf{M}, \mathbf{c} \models \Diamond p \quad \text{iff} \quad \mathbf{M}, \alpha \models \exists c'(Rcc' \& Pc')$$

The right-hand formulas may be computed algorithmically from the left-hand ones. This may be realistic, as linguistic context switches also seem virtually automatic. Even so, these are not quite the McCarthy/Perry equivalences. For, if we put an explicit context variable, we must record the context it denotes. Thus, the explicit version complicates both the syntactic formulation and the semantic setting. Modal correspondences relate what are usually taken to be quite different views of the same models. Thus, they seem a mere tool without linguistic or philosophical import. But in the above light, they lie within one single language, where both modes are available to us in communication. (Mixing these two sides is also a trade mark of recent 'labeled deductive systems': Gabbay 1992.) We do not have to choose: natural language transcends separate formal languages.

Let us analyze the semantics of modal logic a bit further in this light. We find some interesting angles on what is going on. Consider again first-order translations of possible worlds semantics for *modal propositional logic*. Slightly restated, the Perry example looks like this:

$$\mathbf{M}, \mathbf{c} \models p \quad \text{iff} \quad \mathbf{M}, [c := \mathbf{c}] \models Pc$$

The index $\mathbf{c}$ may stand here for a whole package of things (cf. Lewis 1972): time, place, possible world, 'reference group', or whatever else is relevant to determining what is being asserted. Indeed, returning to our earlier translation of the existential modality, modal operators themselves require evaluation dependent on the current context, via accessibility among worlds, witness the following clause:

$$\mathbf{M}, \mathbf{c} \models \Diamond \phi \quad \text{iff} \quad \mathbf{M}, [c := \mathbf{c}] \models \exists c'(Rcc' \& [c'/c]\phi)$$

More subtle forms of context-dependence arise in *modal predicate logics*, which involve interactions between modalities, predication and quantification. This shows in the various relativizations needed for its translations. Consider the following example:

$$\mathbf{M}, \mathbf{c}, \alpha \models \exists x Qjxy \quad \text{iff} \quad \mathbf{M}, [c := \mathbf{c}], \alpha \models \exists x (\underline{D}_c x \& Qcjxy)$$

Here, the domain of quantification gets restricted by the local context **c**, while the same is true for the interpretation of the predicate Q and the individual constant j. The latter effects arise because we relativized the predicate Q to a new argument c. (Working with relational atoms $Qwjxy$ is standard practice. This is equivalent in expressive power to the earlier more cumbersome functional format $I_c(Q)I_c(j)xy$.) But either way, this translation is not forced upon us. It reflects certain decisions that we could have made differently. Consider the following alternative:

$$\mathbf{M}, [c := \mathbf{c}], \alpha \models \exists x(\underline{D}_c x \& I_c(Q)jxy)$$

Here the individual constant j is not relativized to its value in the local context **c**, and it serves rather as an absolute *rigid designator* (Kripke 1972) across contexts. This multiplicity is not a problem. One can argue that both (more) rigid and (more) context-dependent names occur in natural language. Finally, a less obvious choice point in the above semantics emerges here. In the standard semantics of modal predicate logic, one keeps the current world and the variable assignment separate. But a local 'context' may want to package these into one object containing all that is needed for evaluation. Below, we shall show that this observation has surprising technical implications.

In the end, though, the usual technique of 'truth definitions' may not be optimal for a study of context, as it encodes a methodological distinction without a clear correlate in our linguistic practice. In line with our earlier discussion, we may rather want to think of one linguistic medium containing both 'implicit' modal forms and 'explicit' first-order assertions referring to worlds, thus forming the universal language that we all breathe. This language can spawn explicit contexts, or even nested sequences of them, as needed. Moreover, as Buvač & McCarthy observe in their contribution, this language does not require one fixed outer context from which we view all things. The latter would be like the abandoned ideal in classical physics of one absolute space-time frame of reference. Instead, it suffices to know the laws governing the 'coordinate transformations' between different frames of reference and the corresponding 'invariants'. And the latter two notions seem precisely what both Perry and McCarthy are after in 'logical space'.

6   Digression: A Two-Level Context Formalism

Can we take the above ideas a bit further? There are different options for implementing the above ideas as a context logic (cf. Buvač and Mason 1995, Buvač 1995). In the limit, we take a full *two-sorted first-order logic* with separate variables over contexts and over objects. This language can be interpreted in a standard first-order manner, over models with two separate domains. In particular, it contains mixed atoms $Q\mathbf{cx}$ which relate tuples of contexts and worlds. Usually, one only sees cases $Q\mathbf{cx}$ where object predicate Q holds of objects x in a single context c—but more complex cross-contextual comparisons are certainly conceivable ("I am happier *here* than you are over *there*"). But this rich language swamps the intuitive interplay between local and global contexts. Therefore, we work with a more restricted syntax in what follows. Consider an enriched first-order language with object and context variables, but with certain occurrence restrictions on the latter. There are ordinary predicate-object atoms $Q\mathbf{x}$, individual quantifiers $\exists x$ and constants j, but also indexed versions $Q_c\mathbf{x}$, $\exists_c x$ and j_c. The latter are already marked for their context of evaluation, whereas the former are not: by default, they are governed by the current local context. We can make the same distinction for modal operators referring to other contexts: these come in two varieties $\Diamond$ and $\Diamond_c$. This may be implemented in two-sorted models $\mathbf{M}$. Let A be an assignment to object and context variables, $\mathbf{c}$ some local context which is like a standard model in that it provides a domain and interpretation for predicate letters and individual constants. First, we define semantic values for terms in the obvious way. For instance,

$$V_{\mathbf{M}}(A, \mathbf{c}, j) \quad = \quad I_c(j)$$
$$V_{\mathbf{M}}(A, \mathbf{c}, j_{c'}) \quad = \quad I_{A(c')}(j)$$
$$V_{\mathbf{M}}(A, \mathbf{c}, x) \quad = \quad A(x)$$

Here are some self-explanatory truth conditions (we suppress the fixed model $\mathbf{M}$):

$A, \mathbf{c} \models Q j k_{c'} x$ iff $I_c(Q)(V(A, \mathbf{c}, j), V(A, \mathbf{c}, k_{c'}), V(A, \mathbf{c}, x))$

$A, \mathbf{c} \models Q_{c''} j k_{c'} x$ iff $I_{A(c'')}(Q)(V(A, \mathbf{c}, j), V(A, \mathbf{c}, k_{c'}), V(A, \mathbf{c}, x))$

Boolean operations $\{\neg, \&, \vee\}$ *are interpreted as usual*

$A, \mathbf{c} \models \exists x \phi$ iff   *for some* $u \in D_{\mathbf{c}}, A[x := u], \mathbf{c} \models \phi$

$A, \mathbf{c} \models \exists_{c'} x \phi$ iff   *for some* $u \in D_{A(c')}, A[x := u], \mathbf{c} \models \phi$

$A, \mathbf{c} \models \Diamond \phi$ iff   *for some* $\mathbf{c}'$ *with* $R\mathbf{cc}', A, \mathbf{c}' \models \phi$

$A, \mathbf{c} \models \Diamond_{c'} \phi$ iff   *for some* $\mathbf{c}''$ *with* $RA(c')\mathbf{c}'', A, \mathbf{c}'' \models \phi$

This language allows switching back and forth between explicit and implicit context. (Similar modal formalisms occur in Blackburn and Seligman 1995, Goranko 1995.) We can make a local context explicit by tagging on a context variable, and the same mechanism allows us to switch to another context. Conversely, we can fix a context, remove the variables referring to it, and interpret the resulting slimmer formula. Thus, the two basic mechanisms from our opening section find their precise expression. The abstract accessibility relation R for the context modality is just here as a dummy to show the mechanics of the system: it can be replaced by concrete context relations. The proof theory of this language switches between various contexts, just as needed.

How rich should context logics be, to get a handle on the relevant phenomena? Evidently, the above language is just a *fragment* of the full two-sorted first-order logic over contexts and objects mentioned at the start, into which it can be translated. For instance, its context component has a modal flavour. We forbade unrestricted quantification over contexts—leaving only 'bounded' modal variants. Such modal languages have a chance of decidability, even when the full first-order language does not (cf. Andréka et al. 95). There are weaker modal languages than ours. Buvač and Mason 1995 use modalities $[c]$ which reset evaluation in their scope to the context $A(c)$. These do not give us all we want: things become too uniform. For instance, in our semantics, a formula $\exists_{c'} xQjx$, when interpreted in $\mathbf{c}$, gets its j interpreted in $\mathbf{c}$, not in the context $A(c')$. But the latter would happen with its modal approximation $[c']\exists xQjx$. (Adding modal modifiers $[c]j$ on individual constants gives the full power of our system.) In practice, these may be subtle issues. The literature on *temporal semantics* for natural language has seen extensive debates on the power of modalities versus explicit temporal variables needed to capture reference to temporal contexts. (Cf. Kamp 71 on temporal resetters like 'now', and Needham 1975, van Benthem 1977. Oversteegen 1989 proposes co-existence, arguing that both views are needed.) Even so, our context logic models several linguistic phenomena. In language, indexical expressions serve as individual constants referring to the current inner context, while proper names are individual constants referring to the outer context. Also, we can now give formal expression to phenomena of contextualization and de-decontextualization. (Enç 1981 shows the variety of context dependence for common nouns, even inside one single sentence). As for connections with AI systems, our formalism might have to approach a full two-sorted one after all. We may want an explicit first-order calculus reasoning about context accessibility, and then inject its outcomes into context-dependent assertions in the narrower sense. One can make a principled argument that natural language needs this richness, too. Being *semantically universal* in Tarski's sense, it should contain all semantic stances, and hence be rich enough to encompass all (de-)contextualizing translations.

We shall not discuss axiomatization or complexity of this context logic or its modal fragments. Instead, we call attention to two other issues. First, the context domain usually has more structure than that provided above. E.g., when contexts are identified with model triples

(D, I, a), one natural relation is 'domain extension', describing situations where new objects enter into consideration. The logic for their modalities will reflect structural properties of such relations. More generally, we need a richer algebraic theory of natural operations on contexts, in particular, *context merges* of their informational contents and/or referential perspectives. (Many existing theories in the semantic literature already provide some part of this. In a sense, "context" is a new banner on an old battle ground.) Finally, here is another way to go, returning to a previous point. In our system, one might incorporate the variable assignments A *into the contexts* c *themselves*. This would result in a more uniform semantic format $\mathbf{M}, \mathbf{m} \models \phi$ of 'small models' versus 'big models'—- which has some interesting logical repercussions, to be mentioned below.

7 Context: Toward A New Logical Agenda?

For both Perry and McCarthy, context is a central notion in how humans express and handle information. Proper attention to its mechanisms will allow us to better understand how we use language, and to design more efficient systems of information processing. Now, the upshot of our discussion is that 'context' is not so much a new logical primitive, as a new way of looking at existing logical theory, both classical and modal. Thus, we do not think of context as a new ontological category, but rather as a methodological notion. There is no need to duplicate existing theories of sets, possible worlds, or situations, to populate our abstract universe even further. Moreover, several competing methodological notions exist in the logical literature, such as 'state' in dynamic semantics, or 'situation' in situation theory. And under those headings, many of the phenomena dear to our authors are being studied in the current semantic literature. One question, then, is 'paradigmatic'. Which focus works best for understanding the above phenomena? Should we perhaps rearrange the current research agenda under one unifying banner of say 'Context Studies'? I think there is no need yet for such potentially ideological decisions. Further case studies are needed. The notion of context should prove its interest from new *uses* to which it is put, in the analysis of concrete problems. E.g., rather than analyze the metaphysics of context transcendence, one whould state which issue is resolved by introducing such an operation at all. And of these prospective uses, that of 'perspective' seems most novel. Even this narrower methodological focus indeed reveals interesting new patterns in what may seem relatively settled areas of research. Here are a few examples.

Dynamic Semantics

Context change is at the heart of current dynamic semantics (surveyed in Muskens et al. 1997, van Benthem 1996), which describe the dynamic effects of succcesfully evaluating assertions in a model, or incorporating them into some current information state. This perspective suggests dynamic variations (van Benthem and Cepparello 1994) on Tarski's static schema of interpretation for first-order logic, which reads "formula ϕ is true in domain D, given interpretation function I and variable assignment α":

$$\mathbf{D}, \mathbf{I}, \alpha \models \phi$$

Evaluation of a linguistic assertion ϕ may involve changes in all these parameters. Processing generalized quantifiers requires changing domains (cf. the 'context sets' of Westerståhl 1984), processing anaphoric pronouns changes the variable assignment α (cf. Groenendijk and Stokhof 1991), and the predicate interpretation function I may change when processing ambiguous lexical items or questions (van Deemter 1991). This analysis extends to dynamic variations for intensional logics (Cepparello 1995). What stays the same, however, even on the most radical approach, is the linguistic assertion ϕ *itself*. But the above perspective of context change makes even the form of the assertion under evaluation an explicitly modifiable dynamic degree of freedom. More generally, this observation indicates that context theories and dynamic semantics have some promising interfaces, that might be worth elaborating. For instance, systematic changes in linguistic formulation as we cross contexts are indeed 'logical transformations', reminiscent of physical ones. Perhaps, it is time for a semantic Lorentz to stand up ...

Calculus of Contexts

As we have seen, standard model theory itself provides many examples of 'context shift' properties, such as the substitution or relativization lemmas. The full mathematical theory of model relations in the model-theoretic universe is rich and complex. But we can look at the earlier-mentioned modal calculi of context as an attempt at formalizing intuitive and tractable parts of this theory.

Restricting Available Contexts

Our context logic was a rather mainstream modal formalism describing some features of the meta-theory of standard predicate logic. Nevertheless, it suggests some radical departures from the latter. For instance, although contexts may be identified for many purposes with model triples (D, I, a), the converse is much less obvious. Why should *all* such triples be *available* as contexts in our models? Dropping this presupposition leads to a new notion of validity, closer to the 'generalized semantics' for predicate logic of Németi 1993, van Benthem 1995, Alechina 1995, which works with a broader class of first-order models allowing restricted ranges of available variable assignments. Generally speaking, the latter style of modeling induces *decidable* predicate logics. The same may be the natural status for a most general theory of context.

Context and Resources: Interpreting Occurrences

Let us return to our original motivation, viz. the mechanics of changing assertions under interpretation. Compared with actual discourse semantics, Tarski semantics has one more unrealistic idealization. Contexts do not interpret predicate letters or quantifier symbols in a text uniformly, but each *occurrence* one by one (cf. van Deemter 1991). Two occurrences of an existential quantifier may get a different range of individuals, depending on where we are in processing the sentence. Likewise, two occurrences of a predicate symbol may be ambiguous, either blatantly, or via a changed reference set (think of degree adjectives like "small"). Interpretation by occurrences changes the standard format of interpretation, and presumably its logic. Indeed, our conjecture is that the minimal predicate logic of such a scheme is decidable. (For a special case, see Alechina 1995, which considers a modified version of predicate logic where each quantifier $\exists x$ refers to some special domain D_x.)

Redesigning Modal Predicate Logic

Finally, we point out one more curious consequence. Consider again the semantics of modal predicate logic—used to motivate our context language. As is well-known, this logic is fraught with conceptual difficulties, whose full extent is only gradually becoming clear (Ono 1987, Ghilardi 1991). These difficulties all presuppose the usual possible worlds modeling. But in fact, our context logic suggests a redesign here. Instead of using the usual semantic format $\mathbf{M}, \mathbf{w}, a \models \phi$, one may interpret modal predicate logic as follows: $\mathbf{M}, \mathbf{c} \models \phi$, where the context $\mathbf{c}$ has absorbed the individual variable assignment. This redesign will lead to atomic clauses like this:

$$\mathbf{M}, \mathbf{c} \models Qx \qquad \text{iff} \qquad \mathbf{c}(Q)(\mathbf{c}(x))$$

The clause for an existential modality then reads simply as in the propositional case:

$$\mathbf{M}, \mathbf{c} \models \Diamond\phi \qquad \text{iff} \qquad \textit{for some } \mathbf{c}' \textit{ with } R\mathbf{c}\mathbf{c}', \mathbf{M}, \mathbf{c}' \models \phi$$

These truth conditions no longer enforce cross-world identity of objects in evaluation: $\mathbf{c}(x)$ and $\mathbf{c}'(x)$ need not be the same. On the other hand, this move makes validity of all predicate-logical laws unproblematic, unlike what happens in standard modal semantics.

8 Conclusion

What we have discussed here is only a fraction of the themes in McCarthy and Perry. There are many others. For instance, close to the interplay between minimal assertion and (maximal) context is another intuitive principle, namely, of *minimal computation* over our representations. But again, this may lead us into the province of dynamic semantics, which has emerged a number of times by now as a most favored academic trade partner. What we hope to have shown for now is the interest of context as 'logical perspective'.

References

Alechina, N. 1995. *Modal Quantifiers*. Doctoral dissertation, Institute for Logic, Language, and Computation, University of Amsterdam.

Andréka, H., J. van Benthem, and I. Németi. 95. Back and Forth Between Modal Logic and Classical Logic. *Bulletin of the IGPL* 3:685–720. Revised version 'Modal Languages and Bounded Fragments of Predicate Logic' to appear in *Journal of Philosophical Logic*.

Barwise, J. 1989. *The Situation in Logic*. CSLI Publications, Stanford.

van Benthem, J. 1977. Tense Logic and Standard Logic. *Logique et Analyse* 20:41–83.

van Benthem, J. 1984. Correspondence Theory. In *Handbook of Philosophical Logic, Vol. II*, ed. D. Gabbay and F. Guenthner, 167–247. Reidel, Dordrecht.

van Benthem, J. 1995. Modal Foundations for Predicate Logic. Technical Report Report ML–95–07. Institute for Logic, Language and Computation, University of Amsterdam. To appear in E. Orlowska, ed., Logic at Work. Memorial Volume for Elena Rasiowa, Kluwer Academic Publishers, Dordrecht.

van Benthem, J. 1996. *Exploring Logical Dynamics*. Studies in Logic, Language and Information, CSLI Publications, Stanford/Cambridge University Press. North-Holland, Amsterdam.

van Benthem, J., and G. Cepparello. 1994. Tarskian Variations: Dynamic Parameters in Classical Semantics. Technical report. Centre for Mathematics and Computer Science, Amsterdam.

Blackburn, P., and J. Seligman. 1995. Hybrid Languages. *Journal of Logic, Language and Information* 4:3:251–272.

Buvač, S. 1995. Quantificational Logic of Context. In *Proceedings of the Workshop on Modeling Context in Knowledge Representation and Reasoning*. Proceedings IJCAI–13.

Buvač, S., and I. Mason. 1995. Metamathematics of Contexts. *Fundamenta Informaticae* 23:3:263–301.

Cepparello, G. 1995. *Studies in Dynamic Logic.* Doctoral dissertation, Scuola Normale Superiore, Pisa.

van Deemter, K. 1991. *On the Composition of Meaning.* Doctoral dissertation, Institute for Logic, Language and Computation, University of Amsterdam.

Doets, K. 1996. *Basic Model Theory.* CSLI Publications, Stanford.

Enç, M. 1981. *Tense Without Scope: An Analysis of Nouns as Indexicals, On the Composition of Meaning.* Doctoral dissertation, Department of Linguistics, University of Wisconsin. Madison.

Gabbay, D. 1992. Labeled Deductive Systems. Technical report. Department of Computing, Imperial College, London. Institute for Logic, Language and Computation.

Ghilardi, S. 1991. Incompleteness results in Kripke Semantics. *Journal of Symbolic Logic* 56:517–538.

Goranko, V. 1995. Hierarchies of Modal and Temporal Logics with Reference Pointers. *Journal of Logic, Language and Information.*

Groenendijk, J., and M. Stokhof. 1991. Dynamic Predicate Logic. *Linguistics and Philosophy* 14:39–100.

Kamp, H. 71. Formal Properties of "Now". *Theoria* 37:227–273.

Kripke. 1972. Naming and Necessity. *Semantics of Natural Language* 253–355.

Lewis, D. 1972. General Semantics. *Semantics of Natural Language* 169–218.

McCarthy, J. 1993. Notes on Formalizing Context. In *Proceedings IJCAI–93.*

Montanari, A. 1996. *Many-Layered Temporal Logic.* Doctoral dissertation, Institute for Logic, Language, and Computation, University of Amsterdam.

Muskens, H., J. van Benthem, and A. Visser. 1997. Dynamics. In *Handbook of Logic and Language,* ed. J. van Benthem and A.ter Meulen. Elsevier, Amsterdam.

Needham, P. 1975. Temporal Perspective. *Filosofiska Studier 25, University of Uppsala.*

Németi, I. 1993. Decidability of Weakened Versions of First-Order Logic. In *Lecture Notes, Workshop on Algebraization of Logic, Fifth European Summer School in Logic, Language and Information, Lisbon. Handbook of Philosophical Logic, Vol. II.*

Ono, H. 1987. Some Problems in Intermediate Predicate Logics. *Reports on Mathematical Logic 21, 55-67* 21:55–67.

Oversteegen, L. 1989. *Tracking Time.* Doctoral dissertation, Faculteit der Letteren, Rijksuniversiteit Utrecht.

Perry, J. 1993. *The Problem of the Essential Indexical, and Other Essays.* Oxford University Press, New york.

Rosenschein, S., and L. Pack Kaelbling. 1986. The Synthesis of Digital Machines with Provable Epistemic Properties. In *Proceedings TARK,* 83–98. Morgan Kaufmann Publishers, Los Altos. Reidel, Dordrecht.

Westerståhl, D. 1984. Determiners and Context Sets. In *Generalized Quantifiers in Natural Language*, ed. J. van Benthem and A. ter Meulen, 45–71. Foris, Dordrecht.

Zimmermann, Th. E. 1984. Kontextabhängigkeit. In *Semantik: Ein internationales Handbuch der zeitgenössischen Forschung*, ed. D. Wunderlich and A. von Stechow, 156–229. De Gruyter, Berlin.

4

Discourse Preferences in Dynamic Logic

Jan Jaspars and Megumi Kameyama

In order to enrich dynamic semantic theories with a 'pragmatic' capacity, we combine dynamic and nonmonotonic (preferential) logics in a modal logic setting. We extend a fragment of Van Benthem and De Rijke's dynamic modal logic with additional preferential operators in the underlying static logic, which enables us to define defeasible (pragmatic) entailments over a given piece of discourse. We will show how this setting can be used for a dynamic logical analysis of preferential resolutions of ambiguous pronouns in discourse.

1 Introduction

The goal of model-theoretic semantics is to establish an interpretation function from the expressions of a given language to a class of well-understood mathematical structures (models). This enables a formal logical understanding of what an expression means and what its consequences are. For instance, natural language semantics has recently developed a relatively simple *dynamic* model-theoretic understanding of the interplay between indefinite descriptions and anaphoric bindings. These dynamic semantic theories of natural language give model-theoretic explanations of *possible* anaphoric bindings, assuming that additional pragmatics will address the issues of anaphora resolution. A correct dynamic semantic analysis predicts each of the possible refer-

The first author's work was supported by CEC project LRE-62-051 (FraCaS). The second author's work was in part supported by the National Science Foundation and the Advanced Research Projects Agency under Grant IRI–9314961 (Integrated Techniques for Generation and Interpretation). We would like to thank the two anonymous reviewers for helpful comments on an earlier version of the paper.

Computing Natural Language.
Atocha Aliseda, Rob van Glabbeek, and Dag Westerståhl, editors.

ents available in the context, just as a classical logical analysis 'lists' all possible scoping and lexical ambiguities.

Consider the following simple discourses (1) and (2).

(1)   John met Bill at the station. He_1 greeted him_1.

(2)   Bill met John at the station. He_1 greeted him_1.

The two discourses are semantically equivalent. A precise dynamic semantic analysis would treat he_1 and him_1 in both examples as variables that range over the semantic values of John and Bill, with the additional constraint that the referents of he_1 and him_1 are different. This analysis predicts two sets of equally possible bindings. There is, however, a clear preferential difference between the two discourses. There is a preference for the bindings, he_1 = John and him_1 = Bill, in (1), and for the opposite bindings, he_1 = Bill and him_1 = John, in (2).

Preferential effects on discourse interpretations and the entire issue of ambiguity resolution have traditionally been put outside the scope of logical semantics, into the more or less disjoint subfield of 'pragmatics.' This academic focus sharply contrasts with the importance placed on disambiguation and resolution issues in natural language processing (or computational linguistics), where realistic accounts of naturally occurring discourses and dialogues are demanded from application systems. Computational accounts, however, often fall short of logical or model-theoretic formalizations. In artificial intelligence (AI), in contrast, logical formalization of pragmatics, or defeasible reasoning, was brought into the central focus of research at an early stage (see McCarthy and Hayes 1969), and led to the development of nonmonotonic logics.

More recently, there are proposals to incorporate defeasible reasoning within natural language semantics to approximate the class of realistic conclusions of a given sentence or discourse (e.g., Veltman 1991, Lascarides and Asher 1993). In contrast with these specific proposals,[1] we will propose a *general* framework for preferential dynamic semantics, and illustrate how the basic properties of discourse pragmatics exhibited by ambiguous pronouns can be encoded within the framework.

The present framework combines a general model of nonmonotonic logic in Shoham 1988 and a general model of dynamic logic in van Benthem 1991 and de Rijke 1992. In this logical setup, we specify defeasible information and associated entailment relations over a given discourse, and classify the relative stability of conclusions made on the basis of this additional defeasible information. Our paper is about a general frame-

---

[1] Veltman 1991 defines default reasoning in terms of update semantics. Lascarides and Asher 1993 extends Discourse Representation Theory (DRT) with the definition of commonsense entailment given in Asher and Morreau 1991.

work of preferential dynamic semantics that abstracts away from numerous specific possibilities for how to represent utterance logical forms and discourse contexts, and how to actually compute preferences. Since logical formalization of discourse pragmatics is in an early stage of development, we believe that it benefits immensely from an attempt such as here to sort out general meta-theoretical issues from specific accounts.

The paper is organized as follows. Section 2 summarizes the preferential effects on ambiguous discourse anaphoric pronouns. Section 3 presents our basic logical framework. Section 4 illustrates formalisms at work in pronoun interpretation in a first-order discourse logic.

2 Preferences in Ambiguous Pronouns

We summarize, here, the basic properties of preferential effects on discourse semantics. We focus on ambiguous pronouns in simple discourses, and illustrate the properties of dynamicity, indeterminacy, defeasibility, and preference class interactions.

2.1 Discourse Pragmatics as Preferential Reasoning

Most present-day linguistic theorists assume the trichotomy of syntax, semantics, and pragmatics, but there is no single agreed-upon definition of exactly what *linguistic pragmatics* is. Some equate it with 'indexicality', some with 'context dependence', and others with 'language use' (see Levinson 1983). There is also a common pipeline view of the trichotomy, in that pragmatics adds interpretations to the output of semantics that interprets the output of syntax. In this pipeline view, the direct link between syntax and pragmatics is lost.

We take a logic-inspired definition of pragmatics as the *nonmonotonic* subsystem characterized by *defeasible* rules. We also view all defeasible rules to be *preferences*, so the pragmatics subsystem corresponds to a subspace of preferential reasoning, which *controls* the subspace of *possible* interpretations carved out by the indefeasible linguistic rules in the 'grammar' subsystem.[2] From this perspective, pragmatics is not an underdeveloped subcomponent of semantics alone, but a system that combines all the preferential aspects of phonology, morphology, syntax, semantics, and epistemics. There is evidence that these heterogeneous linguistic preferences interact with one another, and also with nonlinguistic preferences coming from the commonsense world knowl-

---

[2]We assume, following the theoretical linguistic tradition, that there is a linguistic rule system consisting of indefeasible rules of morphosyntax and semantics, and call it the 'grammar subsystem'. We also assume that most commonsense rules are defeasible, but leave the question open as to whether there are also indefeasible commonsense rules.

Grammatical Effects:

A. John hit Bill. Mary told *him* to go home.
B. Bill was hit by John. Mary told *him* to go home.
C. John hit Bill. Mary hit *him* too.
D. John hit Bill. *He* doesn't like *him*.
E. John hit Bill. *He* hit *him* back.
K. Babar went to a bakery. He greeted the baker.
    He pointed at a blueberry pie.
L. Babar went to a bakery. The baker greeted him.
    He pointed at a blueberry pie.

Commonsense Effects:

F. John hit Bill. *He* was severely injured.
G. John hit Arnold Schwarzenegger. *He* was severely injured.
H. John hit the Terminator. *He* was severely injured.
I. Tommy came into the classroom. He saw Billy at the door.
    He hit him on the chin. *He* was severely injured.
J. Tommy came into the classroom. He saw a group of boys at the door.
    He hit one of them on the chin. *He* was severely injured.

TABLE 2 Discourse Examples in the Survey

edge. What we have then is a dichotomy of grammar and pragmatics subsystems rather than a trichotomy. Under this view, neither indexicality nor context dependence defines pragmatics since there are both indefeasible and defeasible indexical and context-dependent rules. In fact, in a *dynamic* architecture for discourse semantics, where meaning is given to a sequence of sentences rather than to a sentence in isolation, context dependence is an inherent architectural property supporting the anaphoricity of natural language expressions.

2.2 Basic Properties of Discourse Preferences

We will now motivate four basic properties of discourse preferences with examples of ambiguous discourses with ambiguous pronouns. Kameyama 1996 analyzed a survey result of pronoun interpretation preferences from the perspective of interacting preference classes in a dynamic discourse processing architecture. This analysis identified a set of basic 'design features' that characterize the preferential effects on discourse meaning, and outlined how they combine to settle on preferred discourse interpretations. These basic properties can be summarized as *dynamicity, (in)determinacy, defeasibility,* and *preference class interactions.*

Table 1 shows those examples discussed in Kameyama 1996. In a survey, speakers had to pick the preferred reference of pronouns in the last sentence of each discourse example (shown in italics).[3] Table 2

---

[3]The respondents were told to read the discourses with a 'neutral' intonation, for the survey was intended to investigate only *unstressed* pronouns.

	Answers			$\chi^2_{df=1}$	p
A.	John 42	Bill 0	Unclear 5	37.53	$p < .001$
B.	John 7	Bill 33	Unclear 7	14.38	$p < .001$
C.	John 0	Bill 47	Unclear 0	47	$p < .001$
D.	J. dislikes B. 42	B. dislikes J. 0	Unclear 5	37.53	$p < .001$
E.	John hit Bill 2	B. hit J. 45	Unclear 0	39.34	$p < .001$
K.	Babar 13	Baker 0	Unclear 0	13	$p < .001$
L.	Babar 3	Baker 10	Unclear 0	3.77	$.05 < p < .10$
F.	John 0	Bill 46	Unclear 1	45.02	$p < .001$
G.	John 24	Arnold 13	Unclear 10	2.57	$.10 < p < .20$
H.	John 34	Terminator 6	Unclear 7	16.68	$p < .001$
I.	Tommy 3	Billy 17	Unclear 1	9.33	$.001 < p < .01$
J.	Tommy 10	Boy 7	Unclear 3	0.45	$.50 < p < .70$

TABLE 3　Survey Results

shows the survey results.[4] These and similar examples will be used in this paper.

2.2.1　Dynamicity

We are interested in discourse pragmatics, that is, discourse semantics enriched with preferences, so it is natural to start from where discourse semantics leaves off, not losing what discourse semantics has accomplished with its dynamic architecture and the view of sentence meaning as its context change potential. We thus take *dynamicity* to be a basic architectural requirement in an integrated theory of discourse semantics and pragmatics.[5]

The discourse examples (1) and (2), repeated here, demonstrate the fact that the preferred interpretation of an utterance depends on the preceding discourse context.

(1)　John met Bill at the station. He_1 greeted him_1.

(2)　Bill met John at the station. He_1 greeted him_1.

The two discourses are semantically equivalent. Two male persons, 'John' and 'Bill', engage themselves in a symmetric action of meeting. Both individuals are available for anaphoric reference in the next sentence, and since the two pronouns in *He greeted him* must be disjoint in reference and each pronoun has two possible values, dynamic seman-

---

[4]The $\chi^2_{df=1}$ significance for each example was computed by adding an evenly divided number of the 'unclear' answers to each explicitly selected answer, reflecting the assumption that an 'unclear' answer shows a genuine ambiguity.

[5]There are two levels of dynamicity that affect utterance interpretation in discourse. One is the utterance-by-utterance dynamicity that affects the overall discourse meaning, and the other is the word-by-word or constituent-by-constituent dynamicity that affects the meaning of the utterance being interpreted. In this paper, we will focus on the former.

tic theories predict two equally possible interpretations, John greeted Bill and Bill greeted John. However, these discourses have different *preferred values* for these pronouns. In (1), due to a *grammatical parallelism preference* (exhibited by discourse D in Table 1), the preferred interpretation is John greeted Bill. In (2), the same parallelism preference leads to the reverse interpretation of Bill greeted John.

Dynamic semantics has been motivated by examples such as *A man walks in the park. He whistles.*, where an existential scope extends beyond the syntactic sentence boundary to bind pronouns. Analogously, preferential dynamic semantics would have to account for examples such as (1) and (2), where different syntactic configurations of the same semantic content have different *extended effects* on the preferred interpretation of pronouns.

2.2.2 (In)determinacy

One notable feature of the survey results shown in Table 2 is that the resulting $\chi^2_{df=1}$ significance varies widely. We consider preference to be *significant* if $p < .05$, *weakly significant* if $.05 < p < .10$, and *insignificant* if $.10 < p$ as a straightforward application of elementary statistics. It is reasonable to assume that the statistical significance of a preference corresponds to how determinate the given preference is. Significant preferences are thus unambiguous and determinate, and insignificant preferences indicate ambiguities and indeterminacies. The preferential machinery then must allow both unambiguous and ambiguous preferences to be concluded, rather than always producing a single maximally preferred conclusion.

Preferential reasoning is supposed to resolve ambiguities, however, and unresolved preferential ambiguities make discourses incoherent. It seems reasonable to assume a discourse pragmatic meta-principle that says, *a discourse should produce a single maximally preferred interpretation*. Such a meta-principle is akin to Grice-style maxims of conversation, where a preferred discourse is truthful, adequately informative, perspicuous, relevant, and so forth (Grice 1975). It seems that this kind of a meta-principle is needed to assure that speakers try to avoid indeterminate preferences precisely because the underlying preferential logical machinery does not guarantee determinacy.

We thus identify a basic property of preferential reasoning—preferential conclusions are sometimes *determinate* with a single maximally preferred interpretation, and other times *indeterminate* with multiple maximally preferred interpretations. The latter results in a genuine ambiguity, or incoherence, violating the basic pragmatic felicity condition.

Let us turn to concrete examples. Both discourses (1) and (2) have determinate preferred interpretations due to the grammatical parallelism preference. In contrast, discourse (3) leads to no clear preference because no relevant preferences converge on a single determinate choice. Discourse (3) is thus infelicitous.

(3)   John and Bill met at the station. He greeted him.

2.2.3 Defeasibility

A conclusion is *defeasible* if it may have to be retracted when some additional facts are introduced. This property is also called *nonmonotonicity*, and is the defining property of *preferences*. This property also defines *pragmatic*, as opposed to grammatical, conclusions under the present assumption that grammatical conclusions are indefeasible.

The following continuation of (1) illustrates defeasibility.

(4)   John met Bill at the station. He greeted him. John greeted him
       back.

In (4), the third sentence, with its indefeasible semantics associated with the adverb *back* (as in discourse E in Table 1), forces a reversal of the preferred interpretation concluded after the second sentence. This on-line reversal produces a discourse-level *garden path* effect, analogous to the sentence-level phenomena such as in *The horse passed the barn fell* or *The astronomer married a star*.

Garden path effects are cases of *preference reversal*, which should not be confused with explicit retractions or negations of indefeasible conclusions. The former can be triggered implicitly, whereas the latter must be explicitly asserted. The latter is illustrated by the following discourse-level *repair* example, where the explicit retraction signal *No* negates the immediately preceding assertion, and opens a way for a different fact to be asserted in the next sentence.

(5)   John met Bill at the station. No. He met Paul there.

2.2.4 Preference Classes

When multiple preferences simultaneously succeed, the combined effects are quite unlike the familiar patterns of grammatical rule interactions. When mutually contradictory indefeasible rules both succeed, the whole interpretation is supposed to fail. For instance, *John met Mary at the station. He knows that she loves himself.* leads to no indefeasible interpretation. In contrast, preferences may *override* other preferences that contradict them. Ambiguities persist only when mutually contradictory preferences are equally strong. A logical model of preferential reasoning, therefore, must predict ambiguity resolutions due to overrides.

One type of override is predicted by the so-called Penguin Principle, where the conclusion based on a more specific premise wins (see Lascarides and Asher 1993 for a linguistic application). This principle does not explain all the override phenomena in pragmatic reasoning, however. We must posit the existence of *preference classes* to predict overrides among groups of preferences (Kameyama 1996). We thus distinguish between two kinds of conflict resolutions in pragmatics, one due to the Penguin Principle and the other due to preference class overrides.[6] In this paper, we focus on the interaction between two major preference classes—the *syntactic preferences* based on the *surface structure* of utterances[7] and the *commonsense preferences* based on the *commonsense world knowledge*.

First consider two examples (A and B) in Table 1 repeated here.

(6)   John hit Bill. Mary told him to go home.

(7)   Bill was hit by John. Mary told him to go home.

Discourses (6) and (7) illustrate a syntactic preference—the preference for the main grammatical subject to be the antecedent for a pronoun in the next utterance. Henceforth, this syntactic preference is called the *subject antecedent preference*. In (6), the preferred value of the pronoun *him* is John. In (7), with passivization, the preferred value shifts to Bill. Since passivization does not affect the thematic roles (such as Agent or Theme) of these referents, we conclude that this preference shift is directly caused by the shift in grammatical functions.

Next, consider the following.[8]

(8)   John hit Bill. He got injured.

(9)   The wall was hit by a champagne glass. It broke into pieces.

Discourses (8) and (9) illustrate that the above subject antecedent preference is overridden by a stronger class of preferences having to do with commonsense causal knowledge—in these cases, about hitting causing injuring or breaking.

We thus assume that there are preference classes, or modules, that independently conclude the preferred interpretation of an utterance, and that these class-internal conclusions interact in a certain general overriding pattern to produce the final preference. Table 3 shows the survey

---

[6] Asher and Lascarides 1995 implement a class-level override in terms of a 'meta-penguin principle' forced on rule classes. Their law of 'Lexical Impotence' (p. 96) predicts that discourse inferences generally override default lexical inferences.

[7] This includes both the parallelism and attentional preferences discussed in Kameyama 1996. It was conjectured there that these preference classes may be independent subclasses of a larger 'entity-level' preference class, which is qualitatively different from the 'propositional-level' commonsense preference class.

[8] (8) is a slight variation of F in Table 1. (9) is a variant of Len Schubert's (personal communication) example.

	Synt. Pref.	ComSense Pref.	Semantics	Winner
A.	John	unclear	—	Syntactic Pref.
B.	Bill	unclear	—	Syntactic Pref.
C.	John	unclear	Bill	Semantics
D.	John–Bill	unclear	—	Syntactic Pref.
E.	John–Bill	unclear	Bill–John	Semantics
K.	Babar	unclear	—	Syntactic Pref.
L.	Baker	unclear	—	Syntactic Pref.
F.	John	Bill	—	Commonsense Pref.
G.	John	John/Arnold	—	Commonsense Pref.
H.	John	John	—	Commonsense Pref.
I.	Tommy	Billy	—	Commonsense (but difficult)
J.	Tommy	Boy(/Tommy)	—	??

TABLE 4 Preference Interactions

result analyzed from this perspective of preference class interactions. Based on this analysis, we will model the following general patterns of preference interactions:

- Indefeasible syntax and semantics override all preferences.
- Commonsense preferences override syntactic preferences.[9]
- Syntactic preferences dominate the final interpretation only if there are no relevant commonsense preferences.

The general overriding pattern we identify here is schematically shown as follows, where $\geq$ represents a 'can override' relation:

$$
\begin{array}{ccccc}
\text{Indefeasible} & & \text{Commonsense} & & \text{'Syntactic'} \\
\text{Syntax and Semantics} & \geq & \text{Preferences} & \geq & \text{Preferences}
\end{array}
$$

There are a number of questions about these preference classes. For instance, how do they arise, how many classes are there, and why can some classes override others?[10] In this paper, we simply assume the existence of multiple preference classes with predetermined override relationships, and propose a logical machinery that implements their interactions.

We will now turn to the logical machinery that will be used to model

---

[9]This overriding can be difficult when the syntactic preference is extremely strong. For instance, example I in Table 1 creates an utterance-internal garden-path effect where the first syntactically preferred choice for Tommy is retracted in favor of a more plausible interpretation supported by commonsense preferences.

[10]Kameyama 1996 proposed that there are three preference classes that respectively concern preferred updates of three data structure components of the dynamic context. These three preference classes also seem to correspond with the three classes of *discourse coherence relations* independently proposed in Kehler 1995 to account for the constraints on ellipsis and other cohesive forms. This indicates a potential integration of two apparently unrelated notions—dynamic context data structure components and coherence relations.

pragmatic reasoning with the requisite properties of dynamicity, indeterminacy, defeasibility, and preference class interactions.

3 Dynamic Preferential Reasoning

We have chosen to combine dynamics and preferences in a most general
logical setting in order to achieve logical transparency and theoretical
independence in the following sense. We hope that the logical simplicity
facilitates future meta-logical investigations on the interaction of dynamics and preferential reasoning, and enables applications to a wider
variety of preferential (defeasible) phenomena. We will thus combine
the most general dynamic logical approach and the most general logical
approach to defeasible reasoning we know. The dynamic (relational)
setting consists of the core of the so-called dynamic modal logic in van
Benthem 1991 and de Rijke 1992. Our encoding of defeasibility follows
Shoham's (1988) preferential modeling of nonmonotonic logics.

Subsection 3.1 will outline dynamic modal logic, following Jaspars
and Krahmer's (1996) fragment of the original logic.[11] This part encodes the dynamicity property. Subsections 3.2 and 3.3 will show how
preferential reasoning can be accommodated within this fragment of dynamic modal logic. This addition encodes defeasibility, indeterminacy,
and differentiation of preference classes. Finally, Subsection 3.4 discusses
possible pragmatic meta-constraints on preferential interpretation defin-
able in this logical setting.

3.1 Basic Dynamic Modal Logic

Jaspars and Krahmer 1996 present specifications of current dynamic semantic theories in terms of dynamic modal logic (DML), and show how
DML can be used as a universal setting in which the differences and simi-
larities among different dynamic semantic theories can be clarified. The
underlying philosophy of this unified dynamics is that dynamic theories
evolve from 'dynamifying' an ordinary logic by implementing an order
of information growth over the models of this logic.

To start with, one chooses a *static language* $\mathcal{L}$ to reason about the
content of *information states* S by means of an *interpretation function*:
$[\![.]\!] : \mathcal{L} \longrightarrow 2^S$. This setting most often consists of a (part of) well-known
logic interpreted over a class of well-known models. These models are
then taken to be the units of information, that is, information states,
within the dynamic modal framework. The second (new) step consists of
a definition of an *order of information growth*, $\sqsubseteq$, over these information

---

[11]To be precise, the relational part of this setting is a fragment of the relational
expressivity of original dynamic logic.

states. We write $s \sqsubseteq t$ whenever the state t contains more information than s according to this definition. The conclusive step is the choice of the dynamic language $\mathcal{L}^*$, which essentially comes down to selecting different dynamic modal operators for reasoning about the relation $\sqsubseteq$. The triple $\langle S, \sqsubseteq, [\![.]\!] \rangle$ is also called an $\mathcal{L}$-*information model*.

Conventions. If $M = \langle S, \sqsubseteq, [\![.]\!] \rangle$ is an $\mathcal{L}$-information model, then we write $s \sqsubset t$ whenever $s \sqsubseteq t$ and not $t \sqsubseteq s$. The state t is called a *proper extension* of s. If $T \subseteq S$ then the *minimal states* in T is the set $\{t \in T \mid \forall s \in T : s \sqsubseteq t \Rightarrow t \sqsubseteq s\}$. We will assume that every nonempty subset of information states contains minimal states. Most often, dynamic semantic theories can be described on the basis of information models that satisfy this constraint.

3.1.1 Static and Dynamic Meaning

On the basis of these information models, one can distinguish between static and dynamic meanings of propositions. The *static meaning* of a proposition $\varphi \in \mathcal{L}$ with respect to an $\mathcal{L}$-information model $M = \langle S, \sqsubseteq, [\![.]\!] \rangle$, written as $[\![\varphi]\!]_M$, is the same as $[\![\varphi]\!]$. The reason is that we want to define a dynamic modal extension $\mathcal{L}^*$ on top of $\mathcal{L}$, which requires static interpretation as well ($[\![.]\!]_M : \mathcal{L}^* \longrightarrow 2^S$).

Given the relational structure, that is, the preorder of information growth $\sqsubseteq$, over the information states S, we are able to define a *dynamic meaning* of a proposition. Roughly speaking, the dynamic meaning of a proposition is understood as its *effect* on a given information state $s \in S$.[12] In other words, we wish to define the meaning(s) of a proposition φ *in the context of an information state $s \in S$*: $[\![\varphi]\!]_{M,s}$.

In general, different dynamic interpretations of a proposition φ are defined according to how φ *operates* on an information state. For example, φ might be added to or retracted from an information state, or, in a somewhat more complicated case, φ may describe the content of a revision to an information state. Given such an operation o, we will define the o-meaning of a proposition φ with respect to an information state $s \in S$ (in M): $[\![\varphi]\!]^o_{M,s}$. The proposition φ is the *content* of an operation and o specifies the *type* of operation. In DML, all these operations are defined in terms of the growth relation $\sqsubseteq$.

Jaspars and Krahmer 1996 postulate that in most well-known logics of mental action or change, we need only four basic operation types: *extension* $(+)$ and *reduction* $(-)$, and their minimal counterparts, *update*

---

[12]Note that linguistic actions most often affect the mental state of some chosen agents or interpreters, sharply contrasting with physical actions that affect physical situations, as studied in AI for analysis of so-called frame problems, e.g., Shoham 1988.

$(+\mu)$ and *downdate* $(-\mu)$. Given an information order $\sqsubseteq$ for a given set of information states S, these actions are defined as follows:

(10)
$$\begin{aligned}
[\![\varphi]\!]^{+}_{M,s} &= \{t \in S \mid s \sqsubseteq t,\ t \in [\![\varphi]\!]_M\} \\
[\![\varphi]\!]^{-}_{M,s} &= \{t \in S \mid t \sqsubseteq s,\ t \notin [\![\varphi]\!]_M\} \\
[\![\varphi]\!]^{+\mu}_{M,s} &= \{t \in [\![\varphi]\!]^{+}_{M,s} \mid \forall u \in S : u \in [\![\varphi]\!]^{+}_{M,s}\ \&\ u \sqsubseteq t \Rightarrow t \sqsubseteq u\} \\
[\![\varphi]\!]^{-\mu}_{M,s} &= \{t \in [\![\varphi]\!]^{-}_{M,s} \mid \forall u \in S : u \in [\![\varphi]\!]^{-}_{M,s}\ \&\ t \sqsubseteq u \Rightarrow u \sqsubseteq t\}.
\end{aligned}$$

Furthermore, for every action type o we use $[\![\varphi]\!]^{o}_{M,T}$ as an abbreviation of the set $\bigcup_{s \in T} [\![\varphi]\!]^{o}_{M,s}$ (the o-meaning of φ with respect to T) for all $T \subseteq S$. A special instance of particular importance is the o-meaning with respect to the minimal states in M: $\min_M = \{s \in S \mid \forall t \in S : t \sqsubseteq s \Rightarrow s \sqsubseteq t\}$. We write $[\![\varphi]\!]^{o}_{M,\min}$ instead of $[\![\varphi]\!]^{o}_{M,\min_M}$, and refer to this set as the minimal o-meaning of φ in M. This is the meaning of a proposition with respect to an empty context. We will also use the notation $\min_M T$ for a given subset $T \subseteq S$ of minimal states in T. We assumed above that $\min_S T \neq \emptyset$ whenever $T \neq \emptyset$, and therefore, $[\![\varphi]\!]^{+}_{M,s} \neq \emptyset \Rightarrow [\![\varphi]\!]^{+\mu}_{M,s} \neq \emptyset$ (the same holds for $-$ with respect to $-\mu$).

Dynamic semantic theories most often describe relational meanings of propositions obtained from abstractions over the context. For every operation o, we will call the relational interpretation the o-*meaning* of φ (in M).

(11) $$[\![\varphi]\!]^{o}_{M} = \{\langle s, t \rangle \mid t \in [\![\varphi]\!]^{o}_{M,s}\}.$$

Finally, a dynamic modal extension $\mathcal{L}^*$ of $\mathcal{L}$ can be defined. It supplies unary dynamic modal operators of the form $[\varphi]^{o}$ and $\langle \varphi \rangle^{o}$, whose static interpretations are as follows:

(12)
$$\begin{aligned}
[\![[\varphi]^{o}\,\psi]\!]_M &= \{s \in S \mid [\![\varphi]\!]^{o}_{M,s} \subseteq [\![\psi]\!]_M\} \\
[\![\langle\varphi\rangle^{o}\,\psi]\!]_M &= \{s \in S \mid [\![\varphi]\!]^{o}_{M,s} \cap [\![\psi]\!]_M \neq \emptyset\}.
\end{aligned}$$

For example, a proposition of the form $[\varphi]^{+}\,\psi$ means that extending the current state with φ necessarily leads to a ψ-state, while $\langle\varphi\rangle^{-\mu}\,\psi$ means that it is possible to retract φ from the current state in a minimal way and end up with the information ψ. In this paper, we will discuss only the extension $(+)$ and update $(+\mu)$ meanings of propositions.

Notational conventions. Let C be a set of connectives. Then we write $\mathcal{L}+C$ for the smallest superset of $\mathcal{L}$ closed under the connectives in C. $\mathcal{L} * C$ denotes the smallest superset of $\mathcal{L}$ closed under the connectives appearing in $\mathcal{L}$ and the connectives in C.

3.1.2 Static and Dynamic Entailment

Entailments are defined as relations between sequences of formulae and single formula. The former contain the *assumptions* and the latter are the *conclusions* of the entailments. To make concise definitions, we also define the static and dynamic meaning of a sequence $\varphi_1, \ldots, \varphi_n$, abbreviated as $\vec{\varphi}$, in a dynamic modal language $\mathcal{L}^*$. Let $M = \langle S, \sqsubseteq, [\![.]\!] \rangle \in \mathcal{M}_{\mathcal{L}}$, then

$$(13) \quad [\![\vec{\varphi}]\!]_M = \bigcap_{i=1}^{n} [\![\varphi_i]\!]_M \quad \text{and} \quad [\![\vec{\varphi}]\!]^o_M = [\![\varphi_1]\!]^o_M \circ \ldots \circ [\![\varphi_n]\!]^o_M.^{13}$$

The former part defines the static meaning of $\vec{\varphi}$, and the latter part defines the o-meaning of $\vec{\varphi}$. The o-meaning of $\vec{\varphi}$ is the relation of input/output pairs of consecutively o-executing (expanding, updating,...) φ_1 through φ_n.

We will subsequently write $[\![\vec{\varphi}]\!]^o_{M,s}$ for the set $\{t \in S \mid \langle s, t \rangle \in [\![\vec{\varphi}]\!]^o_M\}$ and $[\![\vec{\varphi}]\!]^o_{M,T} = \bigcup_{s \in T} [\![\vec{\varphi}]\!]^o_{M,s}$ for all $s \in S$ and $T \subseteq S$. We will write $[\![\vec{\varphi}]\!]^o_{M,\min}$ for the minimal o-meaning of the sequence $\vec{\varphi}$.

Definition 1 Let $\mathcal{M}$ be some class of $\mathcal{L}$-information models, and let $\varphi_1, \ldots, \varphi_n, \psi$ be propositions of some dynamic modal extension $\mathcal{L}^*$ of $\mathcal{L}$. We define the following entailments for discourse $\varphi_1, \ldots, \varphi_n$ ($\vec{\varphi}$):

- $\vec{\varphi}$ *statically entails* ψ with respect to $\mathcal{M}$ if $[\![\vec{\varphi}]\!]_M \subseteq [\![\psi]\!]_M$.
- $\vec{\varphi}$ *dynamically entails* ψ according to the operation o (or $\vec{\varphi}$ o-entails ψ) with respect to $\mathcal{M}$ if $[\![\vec{\varphi}]\!]^o_{M,s} \subseteq [\![\psi]\!]_M$ for all $M \in \mathcal{M}$ and s in M.

- $\vec{\varphi}$ *minimally o-entails* ψ with respect to $\mathcal{M}$ if $[\![\vec{\varphi}]\!]^o_{M,\min} \subseteq [\![\psi]\!]_M$ for all $M \in \mathcal{M}$.

We use $\vec{\varphi} \models_{\mathcal{M}} \psi$, $\vec{\varphi} \models^o_{\mathcal{M}} \psi$ and $\vec{\varphi} \models^{\min o}_{\mathcal{M}} \psi$ as abbreviations for these three entailment relations, respectively.

Note that if the modal operators $[\varphi]^o$ are present within the dynamic modal language $\mathcal{L}^*$, then the notion of o-entailment in Definition 1 boils down to the static entailment $\models_{\mathcal{M}} [\varphi_1]^o \ldots [\varphi_n]^o \psi$.

When we think of operations as updates as in the following sections, the minimal dynamic meaning of a sequence $\varphi_1, \ldots, \varphi_n$ is the same as updating the minimal states (the initial context) consecutively with φ_1 through φ_n. This interpretation is the one we will use for *the* interpretation of a discourse or text $\vec{\varphi}$. Of course, as will be the case for most pragmatic inferences, the minimal states of an information model should not be states of complete ignorance. To draw the defeasible conclusions discussed in the previous section, we need to add some defeasible background information. For this purpose we need the following notation. If $\Gamma \subseteq \mathcal{L}^*$, then we write $\mathcal{M}_\Gamma$ for the subclass of models in $\mathcal{M}$ that supports all the formulae in Γ: $\{M = \langle S, \sqsubseteq, [\![.]\!] \rangle \in \mathcal{M} \mid [\![\gamma]\!]_M = S \text{ for all } \gamma \in \Gamma\}$.

---

[13] The operation $\circ$ stands for relational composition. For two relations $R_1, R_2 \subseteq S^2$: $R_1 \circ R_2 = \{\langle s, t \rangle \in S^2 \mid \exists u \in S : R_1(s, u) \ \& \ R_2(u, t)\}$.

The entailment $\vec{\varphi} \models_{M_\Gamma}^{\min +\mu} \psi$ covers the interpretation of a discourse $\vec{\varphi}$ in the context or background knowledge of Γ.

3.2 Simple Preferential Extensions

Shoham 1988 introduced preferential reasoning into nonmonotonic logics. The central idea is to add a preferential structure over the models of the logic chosen as the inference mechanism. This preferential structure is most often some partial or pre-order. A nonmonotonic inference, $\varphi_1, \ldots, \varphi_n \approx \psi$, then says that ψ holds in all the maximally preferred $\vec{\varphi}$-models.

In many nonmonotonic formalisms such as Reiter's (1980) default logic, an additional preferential structure of an assumption set $\vec{\varphi}$ is specified by explicit *default assumptions* Δ, which are defeasible. The central idea is to use 'as much information from Δ as possible' as long as it is consistent with the strict assumptions Φ. We will also encode this maximality preference in our definition. In this paper, we use a preferential operator p to specify the additional defeasible information. A proposition of the form $\mathsf{p}\,\varphi$ refers to the maximally preferred φ-states.

3.2.1 Single Preference Classes

Preferential reasoning can be accommodated within the DML framework by assigning an additional preferential structure to the space of information states. There are essentially two ways to do this. In one method, the preferential structure is added to the static structure over information states ($[\![.]\!]$), and in the other method, it is added to the dynamic structure on these states ($\sqsubseteq$). We take the first, simpler, option in this paper.[14]

As explained in Subsection 2.2.4, the preferential reasoning for anaphoric resolution needs to take different *preference classes* into account. In Subsection 3.3, we will give DML-style definitions for such structures, which will be a straightforward generalization of the following definition of a single preference class.

Definition 2 Extension with a single preference class:

- A *single preferential extension* $\mathcal{L}_\mathsf{p}$ of the static language $\mathcal{L}$ is the smallest superset of $\mathcal{L}$ such that $\mathsf{p}\,\varphi \in \mathcal{L}_\mathsf{p}$ for all $\varphi \in \mathcal{L}$.

---

[14]The latter, more complex, option would be a more balanced combination of dynamic and preferential reasoning because the preferential structure is represented at the same level of information order over which dynamicity is defined. From this perspective, the preferential structuring of models of a given logic that supplies a nonmonotonic component is analogous to dynamifying a logic by informational structuring as described in Jaspars and Krahmer 1996. Such investigations are left for a future study.

- A *preferential* $\mathcal{L}$-model is an information $\mathcal{L}_p$-model $M = \langle S, \sqsubseteq, [\![.]\!] \rangle$, with $[\![.]\!]$ representing a pair of interpretation functions $\langle {}^0[\![.]\!], {}^1[\![.]\!] \rangle$ such that $M_0 = \langle S, \sqsubseteq, {}^0[\![.]\!] \rangle$ and $M_1 = \langle S, \sqsubseteq, {}^1[\![.]\!] \rangle$ are $\mathcal{L}$-information models, and $[\![\varphi]\!] = {}^0[\![\varphi]\!]$ and $[\![\mathsf{p}\,\varphi]\!] = {}^1[\![\varphi]\!]$ for all $\varphi \in \mathcal{L}$.

- If $\mathcal{M}$ is a class of $\mathcal{L}$-information models, then the class of all preferential $\mathcal{L}$ models whose nonpreferential part (0) is a member of $\mathcal{M}$ is called the single-preferential enrichment of $\mathcal{M}$.

- If $\mathcal{L}^* = \mathcal{L} + (*)\, C$, then $\mathcal{L}_p^*$ refers to the language $\mathcal{L}_p + (*)\, C$.

The interpretation function $[\![.]\!]$ consists of an *indefeasible part* ${}^0[\![.]\!]$ and a *defeasible part* ${}^1[\![.]\!]$. Both parts are interpretation functions of the static language: ${}^{0,1}[\![.]\!] : \mathcal{L} \longrightarrow 2^S$. The indefeasible part replaces the ordinary interpretation function, while the additional defeasible part is the 'pragmatic' strengthening of this standard reading. Note that a preferential extension gives us a set of preferred states, allowing both determinate and indeterminate interpretations.

3.2.2 Dynamic Preferential Meaning and Preferential Entailment

Definition (14) illustrates the static and dynamic *preferential* meaning of a sentence φ analogous to the nonpreferential definitions presented in Subsection 3.1.1. The *static preferential meaning* of a sentence φ (in a model M) is written as $\langle\!\langle \varphi \rangle\!\rangle_M$, and the 'dynamic' *preferential meaning* of φ with respect to a given information state (context) s in a model M is written as $\langle\!\langle \varphi \rangle\!\rangle_{M,s}$.

$$(14) \qquad \begin{aligned} \langle\!\langle \varphi \rangle\!\rangle_M &= [\![\mathsf{p}\,\varphi]\!](= {}^1[\![\varphi]\!]) \\ \langle\!\langle \varphi \rangle\!\rangle^o_{M,s} &= \begin{cases} [\![\mathsf{p}\,\varphi]\!]^o_{M,s} & \text{if } [\![\mathsf{p}\,\varphi]\!]^o_{M,s} \neq \emptyset \\ [\![\varphi]\!]^o_{M,s} & \text{otherwise.} \end{cases} \end{aligned}$$

In line with the definitions of Subsection 3.1.1, we write $\langle\!\langle \varphi \rangle\!\rangle^o_M$ for the relational abstraction of $\langle\!\langle \varphi \rangle\!\rangle^o_{M,s}$. Our definition of the preferential dynamic meaning of a discourse $\varphi_1, \ldots, \varphi_n = \vec{\varphi}$ is written as $\langle\!\langle \vec{\varphi} \rangle\!\rangle^o_{M,s}$, and its definition deviates from the way $[\![\vec{\varphi}]\!]^o_{M,s}$ has been defined above because a simple relational composition of the preferential dynamic readings of single sentences does not give us a satisfactory definition. The failure of normal composition in this respect can be illustrated by the following simple abstract example. Suppose $\vec{\varphi} = \varphi_1, \varphi_2$ is a two-sentence discourse with

$$[\![\mathsf{p}\,\varphi_1]\!]^{+\mu}_{M,a} = \{b, c\}, \; [\![\varphi_2]\!]^{+\mu}_{M,1} = \{d\}, \; [\![\mathsf{p}\,\varphi_2]\!]^{+\mu}_{M,1} = \emptyset \text{ and } [\![\mathsf{p}\,\varphi_2]\!]^{+\mu}_{M,2} = \{e\}.$$
(15)

We obtain both $\langle a, d \rangle, \langle a, e \rangle \in \langle\!\langle \varphi_1 \rangle\!\rangle_M \circ \langle\!\langle \varphi_2 \rangle\!\rangle_M$. The second pair ($\langle a, e \rangle$) is composed of maximally preferred readings while the first pair ($\langle a, d \rangle$)

is not. Because these two pairs are both equal members of the composition, such a definition of the preferential meaning of a discourse is not satisfactory.

The two-sentence discourse in this example has four possible readings: (1) composing the two defeasible/preferential readings, (2) composing the indefeasible reading of one sentence and the defeasible reading of the other sentence in two possible orders, and (3) composing the two indefeasible readings. As we said earlier, it is reasonable to use as much preference as possible, which means that (1) should be the 'best' composition, the two possibilities in (2) should be the next best, and (3) should be the 'worst'. We will encode this preferential ordering based on the amount of preferences into the entailment definition. What about then the two possible ways of mixing indefeasible and defeasible readings of the two sentences in the case of (2)? A purely amount-based comparison would not differentiate them. Are they equally preferred?

In addition to the sensitivity to the amount of overall preferences, we hypothesize that the discourse's linear progression factor also gives rise to a preferential ordering. We thus distinguish between the two compositions of indefeasible and defeasible readings in (2), and assign a higher preference to the composition in which the first sentence has the defeasible/preferential reading rather than the indefeasible reading. The underlying intuition is that the defeasibility of information is inversely proportional to the flow of time. It is harder to defeat conclusions drawn earlier in the given discourse. This has to do with the fading of nonsemantic memory with time. Earlier (semantic) conclusions tend to persist, while explicit sentence forms fade away as discourse continues. It seems easier to distinguish (defeasible) conclusions from recently given information than from information given earlier.

We thus take the preferential context-sensitive reading of a discourse $\vec{\varphi} = \varphi_1, \ldots, \varphi_n$ to be the interpretation that results from applying preferential rules as *much* as possible and as *early* as possible. This type of interpretation can be defined on the basis of an induction on the length of discourses:

$$(16) \quad \begin{aligned} {}^{2k}[\![\vec{\varphi}]\!]^o_{M,s} &= [\![\varphi_n]\!]_{M,T} \quad \text{and} \\ {}^{2k+1}[\![\vec{\varphi}]\!]^o_{M,s} &= [\![\mathsf{p}\,\varphi_n]\!]_{M,T} \quad \text{with } T = {}^k[\![\varphi_1, \ldots, \varphi_{n-1}]\!]^o_{M,s}. \end{aligned}$$

Note that $k < 2^{n-1}$ in this inductive definition. ${}^0[\![\varphi_1]\!]_{M,s}$ and ${}^1[\![\varphi_1]\!]_{M,s}$ are given by the $\mathcal{L}$-information model M. The set of states ${}^k[\![\vec{\varphi}]\!]^o_{M,s}$ is called the o-meaning of $\vec{\varphi}$ of *priority* k with respect to s in M. In this way, we obtain 2^n readings of a given discourse. The *preferential o-meaning* of a discourse $\vec{\varphi}$ (w.r.t. s in M) is then the same as the nonempty interpretation of the highest priority larger than 0, and if all these readings are empty, then the preferential o-meaning coincides with the completely indefeasible reading of priority 0.

$$(17) \quad \begin{aligned} \langle\!\langle \vec{\varphi} \rangle\!\rangle^o_{M,s} &= {}^k[\![\vec{\varphi}]\!]^o_{M,s} \\ \text{with } k &= \max\left(\{i \mid {}^i[\![\vec{\varphi}]\!]^o_{M,s} \neq \emptyset, 0 < i < 2^n\} \cup \{0\}\right). \end{aligned}$$

Application of this definition to example (15) yields $\langle\!\langle \varphi_1, \varphi_2 \rangle\!\rangle^{+\mu}_{M,0} = \{e\}$. Definition (17) leads to the following succinct definition of *preferential dynamic entailment*:

$$(18) \quad \begin{aligned} \varphi_1, \ldots, \varphi_n \models^o_{\mathcal{M}} \psi \quad &\Leftrightarrow \quad \langle\!\langle \varphi_1, \ldots, \varphi_n \rangle\!\rangle^o_{M,s} \subseteq [\![\psi]\!]_M \\ &\text{for all } s \text{ in } M, \text{ for all } M \in \mathcal{M}. \end{aligned}$$

This definition says that for every input state of a discourse $\vec{\varphi}$, the maximally preferred readings of the discourse always lead to ψ-states. We write $\vec{\varphi} \models^{\min o}_{\mathcal{M}} \psi$ whenever $\langle\!\langle \vec{\varphi} \rangle\!\rangle^o_{M\,\min} \subseteq [\![\psi]\!]_M$ for all $M \in \mathcal{M}$ (minimal preferential dynamic entailment).

3.3 Multiple Preference Classes

Now we turn to information models of multiple preference classes needed for formalizing the preference interaction in pronoun resolution, as motivated in Section 2. If we assume a linear priority order on these preference classes, then it is not hard to generalize Definition 2 of a single preference class given in Subsection 3.2.1. We will assume such determinate overriding relations among preference classes here.[15]

Definition 3 Extension with multiple preference classes:

- A multiple (m) preferential extension $\mathcal{L}_{\mathrm{p},m}$ of $\mathcal{L}$ is the smallest superset of $\mathcal{L}$ such that $\mathsf{p}_i \, \varphi \in \mathcal{L}_{\mathrm{p},m}$ for all $\varphi \in \mathcal{L}$.
- A multiple (m) preferential $\mathcal{L}$-model is a $\mathcal{L}_{\mathrm{p},m}$-information model $\langle S, \sqsubseteq, [\![.]\!] \rangle$ such that $[\![.]\!] = \langle {}^0[\![.]\!], \ldots, {}^m[\![.]\!] \rangle$ with $M_i = \langle S, \sqsubseteq, {}^i[\![.]\!] \rangle \in \mathcal{M}_{\mathcal{L}}$ for all $i \in \{0, \ldots, m\}$, and $[\![\varphi]\!] = {}^0[\![\varphi]\!]$ and $[\![\mathsf{p}_i \, \varphi]\!] = {}^i[\![\varphi]\!]$ for all $\varphi \in \mathcal{L}$ and $i \in \{1, \ldots, m\}$.
- The class of *m-preferential enrichments* of a class of $\mathcal{L}$ information models $\mathcal{M}$ is the class of all preferential $\mathcal{L}$ models whose indefeasible part (0) is a member of $\mathcal{M}$.

Intuitively, $\mathsf{p}_i \, \varphi$ says that the current state is a preferred state according to the i-th preference class and the content φ. We use a simple generalization of the preferential dynamic meaning given in the previous section for the singular preference setting. For a given discourse $\vec{\varphi} = \varphi_1, \ldots, \varphi_n$, we define $(m+1)n$ readings and define their asso-

---

[15]Kameyama 1996 points out that this is not always the case, but in most cases, strict linearity can be enforced through 'uniting' multiple preference classes of an equal strength into a single one: $[\![(\mathsf{p} \cup \mathsf{p}')\varphi]\!] = [\![\mathsf{p} \, \varphi]\!] \cup [\![\mathsf{p}' \, \varphi]\!]$.

ciated priority in the same manner as in (16). Let $k < (m+1)^{n-1}$ and $T = {}^{k}[\![\varphi_1, \ldots, \varphi_{n-1}]\!]^{o}_{M,s}$. Then ${}^{(m+1)k}[\![\vec{\varphi}]\!]^{o}_{M,s} = [\![\varphi_n]\!]^{o}_{M,T}$ and ${}^{(m+1)k+i}[\![\vec{\varphi}]\!]^{o}_{M,s} = [\![\mathsf{p}_i\,\varphi_n]\!]^{o}_{M,T}$ for all $i \in \{1, \ldots, m\}$. The preferential o-meaning of $\vec{\varphi}$ with respect to a state s in an information model M, $\langle\!\langle\vec{\varphi}\rangle\!\rangle^{o}_{M,s}$, is defined in the same way as for the single preferential case (17): replace 2 with $m+1$.

3.4 Pragmatic Meta-constraints

For most applications, however, this definition is far too general, and we need to regulate the interplay of indefeasible and defeasible interpretations with additional constraints. We discuss some candidates here. Let $M = \langle S, \sqsubseteq, \langle {}^{0}[\![.]\!], {}^{1}[\![.]\!]\rangle\rangle$ be a preferential $\mathcal{L}$-model.

PRINCIPLE 1 (*Realism*) Every preferential φ-state, or $\mathsf{p}\,\varphi$-state, is a φ-state itself:[16]

$${}^{1}[\![\varphi]\!] \subseteq {}^{0}[\![\varphi]\!].$$

This principle is perhaps too strict. In some types of defeasible reasoning, we would like to assign preferential meanings to meaningless or ill-formed input, which would give us the robustness to recover from errors. Such robustness can be expressed in terms of a restriction to nonempty indefeasible readings as follows: ${}^{0}[\![\varphi]\!] \neq \emptyset \Rightarrow {}^{1}[\![\varphi]\!] \subseteq {}^{0}[\![\varphi]\!]$ (Robust Realism).

PRINCIPLE 2 (*Minimal Preference*) In minimal information states, if a proposition has an indefeasible reading, it should also have a preferential reading:

$$[\![\varphi]\!]^{o}_{M,\min} \neq \emptyset \Rightarrow [\![\mathsf{p}\,\varphi]\!]^{o}_{M,\min} \neq \emptyset.$$

The intuition here is that in a minimal state there should be no obstacles that prevent the interpreter from using his preferential expectations or prejudices. In section 4, we will discuss some variants of this principle, which are required to account for certain anaphora resolution preferences.

PRINCIPLE 3 (*Preservation of Equivalence*) Two propositions with the same indefeasible content should also have the same defeasible content:

$${}^{0}[\![\varphi]\!] = {}^{0}[\![\psi]\!] \Rightarrow {}^{1}[\![\varphi]\!] = {}^{1}[\![\psi]\!].$$

---

[16]Compare with the 'realism' principle in Cohen and Levesque 1990: all intended or goal worlds of a rational agent should be epistemically possible. This constraint is often used to distinguish between an agent's desires and intentions.

This principle is not always desirable.[17] For example, in discourses (1) and (2), *John met Bill* and *Bill met John* have the same semantic/indefeasible content, but different pragmatic/defeasible readings. However, some weaker types of equivalence preservation need to play a role for a satisfactory treatment of anaphoric resolution. Such weakenings will also be discussed in section 4.

PRINCIPLE 4 (*Complete Determinacy*) Every preferential φ-extension of a given information state s has at most one maximal element.

$$\#(^{1}[\![\varphi]\!]_{M,s}^{+\mu}) \leq 1 \text{ for all } s.$$

This excludes indeterminacy described in Subsection 2.2.2, prohibiting Nixon Diamonds. Intuitively, it says that pragmatics always enforces certainty. In other words, in cases of semantic uncertainty, pragmatics always enforces a single choice. For example, discourse (3) should always lead to a single pragmatic solution. Therefore, as argued earlier, this constraint is also unrealistic.

4 Toward a Preferential Discourse Logic

We will discuss, here, two different instances of preferential extensions of the DML-setting of the previous section. As we have seen, such an instantiation requires a specification of static and dynamic modal languages and a class of information models. In Subsection 4.1, we will discuss a simple propositional logic, and explain how simple defeasible (preferential) propositional entailments can or cannot be drawn from a set of preferential rules. Our examples will illustrate the defeasible inference patterns commonly called the Penguin Principle and the Nixon Diamond. In Subsection 4.2, we will define a much richer dynamic semantics that integrates the defeasible propositional inferences explained in Subsection 4.1 into anaphora resolution preferences. Such a combination is needed to account for the preferential effects on anaphora resolution. In Subsection 4.3, we will define first-order variants of pragmatic metaconstraints. In Subsection 4.4, we will illustrate the first-order preferential discourse logic with discourse examples with ambiguous pronouns as discussed in Section 2.

---

[17]This principle is often used in nonmonotonic logics. It implies, for example, the dominance of the default conclusions from more specific information ($^{0}[\![\varphi]\!] \subseteq {}^{0}[\![\psi]\!] \Rightarrow {}^{1}[\![\varphi \wedge \psi]\!] = {}^{1}[\![\varphi]\!]$) . If *penguin* $\wedge$ *bird* is equivalent to *penguin*, then Principle 3 makes all the preferential information based on *penguin* applicable, while the preferential information based on *bird* may be invalid for *penguin* $\wedge$ *bird*.

Static Language ($\mathcal{L}$):	A set of *literals*: $I\!P \cup \{\neg p \mid p \in I\!P\}$
Dynamic Language ($\mathcal{L}^*$):	$\mathcal{L} + \{[.]^{+\mu}, \langle . \rangle^{+\mu}\}$
States (S):	arbitrary nonempty set.
Order ($\sqsubseteq$):	arbitrary preorder over S.
Interpretation ($[\![.]\!]$):	A function $\mathcal{L} \mapsto \wp(S)$ such that

$$(i) \quad \forall \varphi \in \mathcal{L}, s, t \in S : s \sqsubseteq t, s \in [\![\varphi]\!] \Rightarrow t \in [\![\varphi]\!].$$
$$(ii) \quad \forall p \in I\!P : [\![p]\!] \cap [\![\neg p]\!] = \emptyset.$$
$$(iii) \quad \forall \varphi \in \mathcal{L} : [\![\varphi]\!] \cap \min_M S = \emptyset.$$

TABLE 5   A Class of Propositional Information Models

4.1   A Simple Propositional Preferential Dynamic Logic

Table 5 gives a DML-specification of a simple dynamic propositional logic. The single preferential extension of this logic illustrates how preferential entailments are established according to the definitions given in the previous section. The information states of this model are partial truth value assignments for the propositional atoms: an atom is either true, false, or undefined. The information order is arbitrary, while the interpretation function is (*i*) *monotonic*, that is, expansions contain more atomic information and (*ii*) *coherent*, that is, expansions contain no contradictory information, and furthermore, there is a constraint that (*iii*) the minimal states have empty atomic content.

Let $\mathcal{M}$ be the class of all single-preferential enrichments of this class of information models subject to both Principle 1 (Realism) and Principle 2 (Minimal Preference) defined in the previous section. Let $\{bird, penguin, can\text{–}fly\} \subseteq I\!P$, and let Γ be the following set of $\mathcal{L}_p^*$-formulae:[18]

$$(19) \quad \begin{aligned} &\{[\mathsf{p}\, bird]^{+\mu}\, can\text{–}fly, \; [\mathsf{p}\, bird]^{+\mu}\, \neg penguin, \\ &[\mathsf{p}\, penguin]^{+\mu}\, \neg can\text{–}fly, [penguin]^{+\mu}\, bird\}, \end{aligned}$$

then:

$(20) \quad bird \approx_{\mathcal{M}_\Gamma}^{\min +\mu} can\text{–}fly \quad$ and $\quad bird, penguin \approx_{\mathcal{M}_\Gamma}^{\min +\mu} \neg can\text{–}fly.$

This entailment is validated by the following derivation for all models $N \in \mathcal{M}_\Gamma$:

$$\begin{aligned} \langle\!\langle bird \rangle\!\rangle_{N,\min}^{+\mu} &= \; {}^1[\![bird]\!]_{N,\min}^{+\mu} \text{ and} \\ \langle\!\langle bird, penguin \rangle\!\rangle_{N,\min}^{+\mu} &= \; {}^1[\![bird, penguin]\!]_{N,\min}^{+\mu} = \\ [\![bird, \mathsf{p}\, penguin]\!]_{N,\min}^{+\mu} &= \; [\![\mathsf{p}\, penguin]\!]_{N,\min}^{+\mu} \subseteq [\![\neg can\text{–}fly]\!]_N. \end{aligned}$$

By definition of the entailment $\approx_{\mathcal{M}_\Gamma}^{\min +\mu}$, we obtain the results of (20).

---

[18]The set Γ prescribes that 'normal birds can fly', 'normal birds are not penguins', 'normal penguins cannot fly' and that 'penguins are birds'.

Next, suppose that $\{republican, pacifist, quaker\} \subseteq I\!P$, and

(21) $\quad \Delta = \{[\,\mathsf{p}\,quaker\,]^{+\mu}\,pacifist,\ [\,\mathsf{p}\,republican\,]^{+\mu}\,\neg pacifist\}.$

Here, the preferential readings of $quaker$ and $republican$ contradict each other. One may expect that we get $quaker, republican \mathrel{\approx}_{\mathcal{M}_\Delta}^{\min+\mu} pacifist$, because the preferences of the last sentence are taken to be weaker in the definition (17). This is not the case, however, because it is possible that a $republican$ cannot be a normal $quaker$ ($[\,republican\,]^{+\mu}\,[\,\mathsf{p}\,quaker\,]^{+\mu}\,\bot$) or vice versa ($[\,quaker\,]^{+\mu}\,[\,\mathsf{p}\,republican\,]^{+\mu}\,\bot$).

If such preferential blocks are removed, we obtain order-sensitive entailments:

(22) $\quad$
$$quaker, republican \mathrel{\approx}_{\mathcal{M}_{\Delta'}}^{\min+\mu} pacifist \quad \text{and}$$
$$republican, quaker \mathrel{\approx}_{\mathcal{M}_{\Delta'}}^{\min+\mu} \neg pacifist \quad,$$

with Δ' denoting the set:

$$\Delta \cup \{[\,quaker\,]^{+\mu}\,\langle\,\mathsf{p}\,republican\,\rangle^{+\mu}\,\top, [\,republican\,]^{+\mu}\,\langle\,\mathsf{p}\,quaker\,\rangle^{+\mu}\,\top\}.^{[19]}$$
(23)

Let $\mathcal{N}$ be the class of double-preferential enrichments of the model given in Table 5 subject to the realism and minimal preference principles on both classes. Let Δ'' be the set

(24) $\quad$
$$\{[\,\mathsf{p}_1\,quaker\,]^{+\mu}\,pacifist,\ [\,\mathsf{p}_2\,quaker\,]^{+\mu}\,quaker,$$
$$[\,\mathsf{p}_2\,republican\,]^{+\mu}\,\neg pacifist\} \qquad\qquad \bigcup$$
$$\{[\,quaker\,]^{+\mu}\,\langle\,\mathsf{p}_i\,republican\,\rangle^{+\mu}\,\top,$$
$$[\,republican\,]^{+\mu}\,\langle\,\mathsf{p}_i\,quaker\,\rangle^{+\mu}\,\top \mid i = 1, 2\} \qquad .$$

The second rule says that the p_2-reading of $quaker$ does not entail any information in addition to its indefeasible reading. In this setting, the two variants in (22) yield the same conclusion dominated by the p_2-reading of $republican$:

(25) $\quad$
$$quaker, republican \mathrel{\approx}_{\mathcal{M}_{\Delta''}}^{\min+\mu} \neg pacifist \quad \text{and}$$
$$republican, quaker \mathrel{\approx}_{\mathcal{M}_{\Delta''}}^{\min+\mu} \neg pacifist \quad.$$

4.2 A First-order Preferential Dynamic Semantics

We will now come to an analysis of the discourses with ambiguous pronouns discussed in Section 2. Typical dynamic semantic analyses of discourse, such as the relational semantics for dynamic predicate logic (Groenendijk and Stokhof 1991) or first-order DRT such as presented,

---

[19] Take $\top = [\,p\,]^{+\mu}\,p$.

for example, in Muskens et al. 1997,[20] do not yield a satisfactory preferential dynamic semantics when we integrate them with the preferential machinery of the previous section. In these types of semantic theories, dynamicity is restricted to the value assignment of variables for interpretation of possible anaphoric links, but to account for anaphora resolution we need a logic that supports a preferential interplay of variable assignments, predicates, names, and propositions. In the terminology of Jaspars and Krahmer 1996, we need to 'dynamify' more parameters of first-order logic than just the variable assignments.[21] To arrive at such extended dynamics over first-order models, we will establish a combination of the 'ordinary' dynamics-over-assignments semantics with the models of information growth used in possible world semantics for classes of constructive logics.[22]

Let us first present the class of our information models. The basic linguistic ingredients are the same as for first-order logic: Con a set of constants, Var a disjoint countably infinite set of variables, and for each natural number n a set of n-ary predicates Pred^n. The static language is the same as for first-order logic except for quantifiers and negation. The dynamic language supplies the formalism with dynamic modal operators $[.]^{+\mu}$ and $\langle.\rangle^{+\mu}$:

$$
\begin{aligned}
\mathsf{Atoms} &= \{Pt_1 \ldots t_n \mid P \in \mathsf{Pred}^n, t_i \in \mathsf{Con} \cup \mathsf{Var}\} \\
&\quad \cup \{t_1 = t_2 \mid t_i \in \mathsf{Con} \cup \mathsf{Var}\} \\
\mathcal{L} &= \mathsf{Atoms} + \{\wedge, \vee, \bot\} \\
\mathcal{L}^* &= \mathcal{L} * \{[.]^{+\mu}, \langle.\rangle^{+\mu}\}.
\end{aligned}
$$

(26)

Table 6 presents the intended $\mathcal{L}$-information models. The growth of the information order $\sqsubseteq$ is subject to three constraints. The first one (i) says that all the parameters of first-order logic, that is, the domains, interpretation of predicates and constants, and the variable assignments, grow with the information order. The other two constraints seem unorthodox. The second constraint (ii) ensures the freedom of variables in this setting. It tells us that in each state the range of a 'fresh' variable is unlimited, that is, it may have the value of each current or 'future' in-

---

[20] Jaspars and Krahmer 1996 discusses the DML-specification of this semantics for DRT. On the basis of these DML-specifications, one can transfer the present definitions of preferential dynamic entailment to a range of dynamic semantics.

[21] van Benthem and Cepparello 1994 discusses such further dynamification. Groenendijk et al. 1996 proposes a semantic theory that combines 'propositional' and 'variable' dynamics, introducing a dynamic semantics over assignment-world pairs. It may be possible to obtain a suitable preferential extension of this type of semantics for our purposes as well.

[22] See Troelstra and Van Dalen 1988 or Fitting 1969 for the case of intuitionistic logic.

States (S):	A collection of quadruples $s = \langle D^s, I^s_p, I^s_c, I^s_v \rangle$ with D^s a nonempty set of *individuals*, $I^s_p : \mathsf{Pred}^n \longrightarrow \wp((D^s)^n)$ the *local interpretation of predicates*, $I^s_c : \mathsf{Con} \rightsquigarrow D$ a *partial local interpretation of constants*, and $I^s_v : \mathsf{Var} \rightsquigarrow D$ a *partial variable assignment*.
Order ($\sqsubseteq$):	A preorder over S such that
	(i) For all $s, t \in S$ if $s \sqsubseteq t$ then $D^s \subseteq D^t$, $I^s_p(P) \subseteq I^t_p(P)$ for all predicates P, $I^s_c(\mathsf{c}) = I^t_c(\mathsf{c})$ for all $\mathsf{c} \in \mathsf{Dom}(I^s_c)$ and $I^s_v(x) = I^t_v(x)$ for all $x \in \mathsf{Dom}(I^s_v)$.
	(ii) For all $s, t \in S$ if $s \sqsubseteq t$, $d \in D^t$ and $x \in \mathsf{Var} \setminus \mathsf{Dom}(I^s_v)$, then there exists $u \in S$ such that $s \sqsubseteq u$ and $D^t = D^u$, $I^t_p = I^u_p$, $I^t_c = I^u_c$, $\mathsf{Dom}(I^u_v) = \mathsf{Dom}(I^s_v) \cup \{x\}$ and $I^u_v(x) = d$.
	(iii) For all $s \in \min_M S$: $I^s_p(P) = \emptyset$ for all predicates P and $\mathsf{Dom}(I^s_c) = \mathsf{Dom}(I^s_v) = \emptyset$.
Interpretation ($[\![.]\!]$):	$[\![Pt_1 \ldots t_n]\!] = \{s \in S \mid \langle I^s_t(t_1), \ldots, I^s_t(t_n) \rangle \in I^s_p(P)\}$, $[\![t_1 = t_2]\!] = \{s \in S \mid I^s_t(t_1) = I^s_t(t_2)\}$, $[\![\varphi \wedge \psi]\!] = [\![\varphi]\!] \cap [\![\psi]\!]$, $[\![\varphi \vee \psi]\!] = [\![\varphi]\!] \cup [\![\psi]\!]$, $[\![\bot]\!] = \emptyset$.

TABLE 6   A Class of First-order Information Models

dividual. This means that for every individual d in an extension t, every variable x that does not yet have an assigned value may be assigned the value d in a state containing the same information as t. This constraint differentiates the roles of constants and variables in this setting. The last constraint (iii) says that the minimal information states do not contain atomic information. It was also used for propositional information models in Subsection 4.1.

The interpretation function is more or less standard. Verification of an atomic sentence requires determination of all the present terms, also for identities.

Quantification can be defined by means of the dynamic modal operators. For example, (27) means that the *Meet*-relation is symmetric and *Greet*-relation is irreflexive.

(27) $[\, Meet\, xy\,]^{+\mu}\, Meet\, yx$ and $[\, Greet\, xy\,]^{+\mu}\, [x = y]^{+\mu} \bot$.

Ordinary universal quantification can be defined by using identity and extension modality: $\forall x \varphi = [x = x]^+ \varphi.$[23] Negation can also be defined by means of a dynamic modal operator: $\neg \varphi = [\varphi]^+ \bot.$[24] A typical

---

[23] Note that to get the proper universal reading here, we need to be sure that x is a fresh variable (e.g., in the minimal states).

[24] A proper definition of existential quantification does not seem feasible since $\langle x = x \rangle^{+\mu} \varphi$ is not persistent. A better candidate is $\neg \forall x \neg \varphi$, which behaves persistently. For $\bot$ we may take $\langle x = x \rangle^+ (x = x)$.

(singular) preferential sentence would be

$$(28) \qquad [\mathsf{p} \, Meet \, xy]^{+\mu} \, [\mathsf{p} \, Greet \, uv]^{+\mu} \, (u = x \wedge v = y),$$

which means that the concatenation of the preferential reading of a *Meeting* and a *Greeting* pair makes the variables match according to the grammatical parallelism preference.[25]

4.3 First-order Constraints for Preferential Dynamic Reasoning

To model the preferential effects on ambiguous pronouns discussed in Section 2, we need to postulate several first-order variants of the pragmatic meta-constraints discussed in Subsection 3.4. The first-order expressivity of the languages $\mathcal{L}$ and $\mathcal{L}^*$ given in (26) and the fine structure of the information models presented in Table 6 enable us to calibrate these meta-constraints for preferential interpretation on first-order discourse representations.

We will adopt only Principle 1 (Realism) in its purely propositional form. Three other constraints that we will impose on preferential interpretation regulate some 'harmless' interplay of preferences and terms. Let $M = \langle S, \sqsubseteq, [\![.]\!] \rangle$ be a preferential $\mathcal{L}$-model with $[\![.]\!] = \langle {}^0[\![.]\!], {}^1[\![.]\!] \rangle$.

To begin with, fresh variables have no content, and therefore, we do not allow them to block preferential interpretation. In other words, a proposition that contains only fresh variables as terms always has a preferential $+\mu$-reading whenever it has an indefeasible $+\mu$-meaning. In fact, this is a variant of Principle 2, the principle of minimal preference.

PRINCIPLE 5 (*Minimal Preference for Fresh Variables*) Let s be an information state in an information model of the type described in Table 6. If $\mathrm{Dom}(I_v^s)$ has an empty intersection with the variables occurring in a given proposition φ, and no constants occur in φ, then

$$[\![\varphi]\!]_{M,s}^{+\mu} \neq \emptyset \Rightarrow [\![\mathsf{p} \, \varphi]\!]_{M,s}^{+\mu} \neq \emptyset.$$

The two other constraints for first-order discourses are obtained by weakening Principle 3 (Preservation of Equivalence). Although this principle itself is too strong, we would like to have some innocent logical transparency of the preferential operator. We thus postulate Principles 6 and 7.

PRINCIPLE 6 (*Preservation under Renaming Fresh Variables.*) Preferential readings should be maintained when fresh variables are replaced

---

[25] A general implementation of the parallelism preference would require a second-order scheme.

by other fresh variables:

$$\forall x, y \in \mathsf{Var} \setminus \mathsf{Dom}(I_v^s) : s \in [\![\mathsf{p}\,\varphi]\!]_M \Leftrightarrow s \in [\![\mathsf{p}\,\varphi[x/y]]\!]_M.$$

PRINCIPLE 7 (*Preservation of Identities.*) Preferential readings should be insensitive to substitutions of equals:

$$\forall t_1, t_2 \in \mathsf{Var} \cup \mathsf{Con} : s \in [\![\mathsf{p}\,\varphi \wedge t_1 = t_2]\!]_M \Leftrightarrow s \in [\![\mathsf{p}\,\varphi[t_1/t_2]]\!]_M.$$

4.4 Preferential Dynamic Disambiguation of Pronouns

We will now account for the discourse examples with ambiguous pronouns discussed in Section 2 using the first-order preferential discourse logic defined here.

4.4.1 Single-preferential Structure

We will first examine the single-preferential structure of the 'John met Bill' sentences (1)–(4). Assume the single-preferential extensions $\mathcal{M}$ of the models presented in Table 6 subject to Principles 1, 5, 6, and 7. This model, together with the background information Γ containing (27) and (28), yields the intended defeasible conclusions as follows:

(29) $$\begin{array}{ll} x = \mathsf{j} \wedge y = \mathsf{b}, \mathit{Meet}\,xy, \mathit{Greet}\,uv & \approx_{\mathcal{M}_\Gamma}^{\min+\mu} \quad (u = \mathsf{j} \wedge v = \mathsf{b}) \\ x = \mathsf{b} \wedge y = \mathsf{j}, \mathit{Meet}\,xy, \mathit{Greet}\,uv & \approx_{\mathcal{M}_\Gamma}^{\min+\mu} \quad (u = \mathsf{b} \wedge v = \mathsf{j}). \end{array}$$

This class also entails the invalidity of this kind of a determinate resolution for the 'John and Bill met'-case (3):

(30) $$\begin{array}{c} x = \mathsf{j} \wedge y = \mathsf{b}, \\ \mathit{Meet}\,xy \wedge \mathit{Meet}\,yx, \mathit{Greet}\,uv \quad \not\approx_{\mathcal{M}_\Gamma}^{\min+\mu} \quad (u = \mathsf{j} \wedge v = \mathsf{b}). \end{array}$$

The underlying reason is that the preferential meaning of $\mathit{Meet}\,xy \wedge \mathit{Meet}\,yx$ may be different from that of $\mathit{Meet}\,xy$ or $\mathit{Meet}\,yx$, although these three sentences all have the same indefeasible meaning in $\mathcal{M}_\Gamma$.

For discourse (1) extended with the sentence *John greeted back* in (4), the defeasible conclusion of the first discourse in (29) will be invalid over $\mathcal{M}_\Gamma$:

(31) $$\begin{array}{c} x = \mathsf{j} \wedge y = \mathsf{b}, \\ \mathit{Meet}\,xy, \mathit{Greet}\,uv, \mathit{Greet}\,xu \quad \not\approx_{\mathcal{M}_\Gamma}^{\min+\mu} \quad (u = \mathsf{j} \wedge v = \mathsf{b}). \end{array}$$

The reason is that for every model $M \in \mathcal{M}_\Gamma$:

(32) $$\begin{array}{c} \forall s \in S : s \in \langle\!\langle x = \mathsf{j} \wedge y = \mathsf{b}, \mathit{Meet}\,xy, \mathit{Greet}\,uv \rangle\!\rangle_{M,\min}^{+\mu} \Rightarrow \\ [\![\mathit{Greet}\,xu]\!]_{M,s}^{+\mu} = \emptyset. \end{array}$$

4.4.2 Double-preferential Structure

We will now illustrate how the overriding effects of commonsense preferences illustrated in (8) and (9) come about in a double-preferential extension of the DML-setting in Table 6. In these cases, we hypothesized that the commonsense preferences about hitting / injuring / breaking override the syntactic preferences underlying the 'John met Bill' examples (1)–(4). We postulate the following double-preferential background for the 'hitting' scene:

$$(33) \qquad \begin{aligned} &[\mathsf{p}_1 \, Hit \, xy]^{+\mu} [\mathsf{p}_1 \, Injured \, v]^{+\mu} \, v = x \quad \text{and} \\ &[\mathsf{p}_2 \, Hit \, xy]^{+\mu} [Injured \, v]^{+\mu} \, v = y \quad . \end{aligned}$$

The p_2-class is associated with commonsense preferences with a higher preferential rank, while the p_1-class is associated with 'syntactic' preferences with a lower preferential rank. Note that we take the commonsense impact of the word *Hit* so strongly that every *Injured v*-continuation—not only the preferred readings of this sentence—leads to the defeasible conclusion that the hittee is the one who must be injured.

The above double-preferential account also enables a formal distinction among discourses F (same as (8) involving Bill), G (involving Schwarzenegger), and H (involving the Terminator) in Table 2, whose differences are exhibited in the survey results presented in Table 3.

Let $\mathcal{N}$ be the class of double-preferential enrichments of the models of Table 6 satisfying the same principles as $\mathcal{M}$ for both preference classes. When Δ represents the set containing the two preferential update rules given in (33), we obtain a determinate preference for F:

$$(34) \qquad x = \mathsf{j} \wedge y = \mathsf{b}, Hit \, xy, Injured \, v \underset{\mathcal{N}_\Delta}{\overset{\min \, +\mu}{\approx}} v = \mathsf{b}.$$

Let Δ' be the extension of Δ enriched with the following additional commonsense rules, where sch denotes Schwarzenegger:

$$(35) \qquad [\mathsf{p}_2 \, Injured \, x]^{+\mu} [x = \mathsf{sch}]^{+\mu} \perp.$$

This rule says that if something is injured, then it is not expected to be Schwarzenegger. We then obtain a case of indeterminacy for G:

$$(36) \qquad \begin{aligned} &x = \mathsf{j} \wedge y = \mathsf{sch}, Hit \, xy, Injured \, v \underset{\mathcal{N}_{\Delta'}}{\overset{\min \, +\mu}{\not\approx}} v = \mathsf{sch} \text{ and} \\ &x = \mathsf{j} \wedge y = \mathsf{sch}, Hit \, xy, Injured \, v \underset{\mathcal{N}_{\Delta'}}{\overset{\min \, +\mu}{\not\approx}} v = \mathsf{j}. \end{aligned}$$

Let Δ'' be the union of Δ and the following additional rules, where the constant tm denotes the Terminator:

$$(37) \qquad [\mathsf{j} = \mathsf{tm}]^{+\mu} \perp \text{ and } [Injured \, \mathsf{tm}]^{+\mu} \perp.$$

The second sentence says that the Terminator cannot be injured. This background information establishes the preferred meaning of H:

$$(38) \qquad x = \mathsf{j} \wedge y = \mathsf{tm}, Hit \, xy, Injured \, v \underset{\mathcal{N}_{\Delta''}}{\overset{\min \, +\mu}{\approx}} v = \mathsf{j}.$$

Substitution of $\Theta = \Delta' \cup \Delta''$ for Δ in (34), for Δ' in (36) and for Δ'' in (38) yields the same conclusions as above. In summary, if Θ was our background knowledge, then the discourse F predicts that Bill is injured, while G yields indeterminacy in its preferential meaning. Discourse H preferentially entails that John is injured.

5 Conclusions and Future Prospects

As a general logical basis for an integrated model of discourse semantics and pragmatics, we have combined dynamics and preferential reasoning in a dynamic modal logic setting. This logical setting encodes the basic discourse pragmatic properties of dynamicity, indeterminacy, defeasibility, and preference class interactions posited in an earlier linguistic analysis of the preferential effects on ambiguous pronouns. It also provides a logical architecture in which to implement a set of meta-constraints that regulates the general interplay of defeasible and indefeasible static and dynamic interpretation. We have given a number of such meta-constraint candidates here. Further logical and empirical investigations are needed before we can choose the exact set of constraints we need.

We demonstrated how a general model theory of dynamic logic can be enriched with a preferential structure to result in a relatively simple preferential model theory. We defined the preferential dynamic entailments over given pieces of discourse, which predict that preferential information is used as much as possible and as early as possible to conclude discourse interpretations. That is, earlier defeasible conclusions are harder to defeat than more recent ones. We have also defined a logical machinery for predicting overriding relationships among preference classes. Overriding takes place when later indefeasible information defeats earlier preferential conclusions, or when a reading corresponding to a preference class of a higher priority becomes empty and a lower preference class takes over. These preference class overrides give rise to conflict resolutions that are not predictable from straightforward applications of the Penguin Principle.

Although our focus is on pronoun resolution preferences in this paper, we hope that our logical machinery is also adequate for characterizing the conflict resolution patterns among various preferences and preference classes relevant to a wider range of discourse phenomena. The present perspective of preference interactions assumes that preferences belong to different classes, or modules, and that there are certain common conflict resolution patterns *within* each class and *across* different classes. Class-internal preference interactions yield either determinate or indeterminate preferences. Class-external preference interactions are dictated by certain preexisting class-level overriding relations, according to which the conflicts among the respective conclusions coming from each preference class are either resolved (by class-level overrides), ending up with the preferential conclusions of the highest preference class (whether it is determinate or indeterminate), or unresolved, leading to mixed-class preferential ambiguities. We would like to investigate the applicability of this perspective to a wider range of discourse phenomena.[26]

The present logical characterization of preferential dynamics may be extended and/or revised in two major areas. One is the application of actions other than updates, $+\mu$. For example, discourse-level repairs as in (5) also require reductions, $-$, and/or downdates, $-\mu$. The other is the relational definition of preferences on the basis of an additional structuring of the information order $\sqsubseteq$ instead of the static interpretation function $[\![.]\!]$. Such an alternative definition would enable us to implement 'graded' preferences (Delgrande 1988), that is, every state gets a certain preferential status with respect to a proposition. In our paper, states were simply declared to be preferential or nonpreferential with respect to a proposition. Graded preferences may be required for fine-tuning and coordinating the overall discourse pragmatics. A question related to this topic is whether the use of graded preferences would make the setting of multiple preference classes superfluous.

We might also be able to extend the framework to cover on-line sentence processing pragmatics, where the word-by-word or constituent-by-constituent dynamicity affects the meaning of the utterance being interpreted. The utterance-internal garden path and repair phenomena will then be treated analogously to the discourse-level counterparts.

References

Asher, Nicholas, and Alex Lascarides. 1995. Lexical Disambiguation in a Discourse Context. *Journal of Semantics* 12(1):69–108. Special Issue on Lexical Semantics, Part I.

Asher, Nicholas, and Michael Morreau. 1991. Commonsense Entailment: A Modal Theory of Non-Monotonic Reasoning. In *Logics in AI / JELIA90*, ed. J. van Eijck. Lecture Notes in Artificial Intelligence, Vol. 478, 1–30. Heidelberg: Springer Verlag.

van Benthem, Johan. 1991. *Language in Action*. Studies in Logic and the Foundations of Mathematics, Vol. 130. Amsterdam: North Holland.

van Benthem, Johan, and Giovanna Cepparello. 1994. Tarskian Variations; Dynamic Parameters in Classical Logic. Technical Report CS-R9419. Amsterdam: CWI.

---

[26]It is encouraging that the recent spread of Optimality Theory from phonology (Prince and Smolensky 1993) to syntax (e.g., MIT Workshop on Optimality in Syntax, 1995) seems to indicate the descriptive adequacy of the fundamental preference interaction scheme, where potentially conflicting defeasible conclusions compete for the 'maximal harmony.'

Cohen, Phil, and Hector Levesque. 1990. Intention is choice with commitment. *Artificial Intelligence Journal* 42:213–261.

Delgrande, J. 1988. An approach to default reasoning based on first-order conditional logic. *Artificial Intelligence Journal* 36:63–90.

Fitting, Melvin. 1969. *Intuitionistic Logic: Model Theory and Forcing.* Studies in Logic and the Foundations of Mathematics. Amsterdam: North Holland.

Grice, H. Paul. 1975. Logic and Conversation. In *Speech Acts: Syntax and Semantics*, ed. P. Cole and J. Morgan. 41–58. New York: Academic Press.

Groenendijk, J., M. Stokhof, and F. Veltman. 1996. Coreference and Modality. In *The Handbook of Contemporary Semantic Theory*, ed. Shalom Lappin. 179–213. Oxford, UK: Blackwell.

Groenendijk, Jeroen, and Martin Stokhof. 1991. Dynamic Predicate Logic. *Linguistics and Philosophy* 14:39–100.

Jaspars, Jan, and Emiel Krahmer. 1996. A programme of modal unification of dynamic theories. In *Proceedings of the Tenth Amsterdam Colloquium*, ed. P. Dekker and M. Stokhof. 425–444. Amsterdam: ILLC.

Kameyama, Megumi. 1996. Indefeasible Semantics and Defeasible Pragmatics. In *Quantifiers, Deduction, and Context*, ed. M. Kanazawa, C. Piñon, and H. de Swart. 111–138. Stanford, CA: CSLI.

Kehler, Andrew. 1995. *Interpreting Cohesive Forms in the Context of Discourse Inference.* Doctoral dissertation, Harvard University, Cambridge, MA, June. TR-11-95, Center for Research in Computing Technology.

Lascarides, Alex, and Nicholas Asher. 1993. Temporal Interpretation, Discourse Relations, and Commonsense Entailment. *Linguistics and Philosophy* 16:437–493.

Levinson, Stephen C. 1983. *Pragmatics.* Cambridge Textbooks in Linguistics. Cambridge, U.K.: Cambridge University Press.

McCarthy, John, and Patrick Hayes. 1969. Some Philosophical Problems from the Standpoint of Artificial Intelligence. In *Machine Intelligence*, ed. B. Meltzer and D. Michie. 463–502. Edinburgh: Edinburgh University Press.

Muskens, Reinhard, Johan Van Benthem, and Albert Visser. 1997. Dynamics. In *Handbook of Logic and Language*, ed. Johan Van Benthem and Alice ter Meulen. 587–648. Elsevier Science.

Prince, A., and P. Smolensky. 1993. Optimality Theory: Constraint Interaction in Generative Grammar. Technical Report 2. New Brunswick, NJ: Center for Cognitive Science, Rutgers University.

Reiter, Raymond. 1980. A logic for default reasoning. *Artificial Intelligence Journal* 13:81–132.

de Rijke, Maarten. 1992. A System of Dynamic Modal Logic. Technical Report 92-170. Stanford, CA: CSLI. to appear in the *Journal of Philosophical Logic*.

Shoham, Yoav. 1988. *Reasoning About Change: Time and Causation from the Standpoint of Artificial Intelligence*. The MIT Press Series in Artificial Intelligence. Cambridge, MA: MIT Press.

Troelstra, Anne, and Dirk Van Dalen. 1988. *Constructivism in Mathmatics, volume I*. Studies in Logic and the Foundations of Mathematics. Amsterdam: North Holland.

Veltman, Frank. 1991. Defaults in Update Semantics. Technical Report LP-91-02. Department of Philosophy, University of Amsterdam. To appear in the *Journal of Philosophical Logic*.

5

Polarity, Predicates and Monotonicity

Víctor Sánchez Valencia

1 Introduction

In this paper we shall be concerned with a subclass of the expressions that, since Klima 1964, have been called *affective*. The property of affective expressions which will be our concern here is that they license negative polarity items . This point is illustrated by the following sentences in which the negative polarity items *any* and *ever* are triggered by the affective predicates *inconceivable, unlikely, surprised, ashamed, stupid* and *reluctant*:

(1)   a. It is inconceivable that he could do *any* more
      b. It is unlikely that he will do *any* more
      c. I am surprised that he *ever* speaks to her
      d. He was ashamed to take *any* more money
      e. He was stupid to become *any* heavier
      f. He was reluctant to see *any* more patients

To complement this illustration, notice that the natural counterparts of these sentences are not felicitous utterances in English:

(2)   a. It is conceivable that he could do *any* more
      b. It is likely that he will do *any* more
      c. I expected that he *ever* speaks to her
      d. He was proud to take *any* more money

The research reported here has been carried out within the framework of the PIO-NIER project 'Reflections of Logical Patterns in Language Structure and Language Use', which is financed by NWO, (the Dutch Organisation for Scientific Research), and the University of Groningen. I am also in debt to Johan van Benthem, Bill Ladusaw and an anonymous reviewer of this volume for helpful comments.

Computing Natural Language.
Atocha Aliseda, Rob van Glabbeek, and Dag Westerståhl, editors.
Copyright © 1998, Stanford University.

    e. He was wise to become *any* heavier

    f. He was willing to see *any* more patients

The difference in felicity that shows up in the above sets of sentences is something that needs to be explained by a linguistic theory. In fact, Klima's previously mentioned work is an early attempt to accomodate polarity phenomena within the scope of formal syntax. A recent example of a syntactic account of polarity is Progovac 1994. The problem of accounting for the licensing behaviour of polarity triggers was gradually transformed into an interesting question for semantics. The semantic trail begins probably with Baker 1970, through Fauconnier 1975 to Ladusaw 1979. Ladusaw's account has been rather successful. According to Bach 1989 it is 'a promising model-theoretic account of the licensing conditions for polarity items'. This account, however, is not without problems as one can discover by consulting Linebarger 1980. Affective predicates are important in this regard. They are judged to be problematic for Ladusaw's semantic theory and they are, therefore, used as evidence against it. I happen to disagree with this judgement and I argue in this paper that, in spite of appearances, the semantic behaviour of a considerable number of affective predicates fits very well with Ladusaw's views: negative polarity triggers are downward monotone expressions. To impress this idea upon the reader is the main goal of this paper.

After having described my objectives let me describe the structure of this paper. In the second section I discuss the problems that affective predicates pose to Ladusaw's Hypothesis. The third section contains the version of monotonicity that circumvents the earlier mentioned difficulties. The clue to my proposal is that many affective predicates are gradable adjectives, that is, adjectives associated with comparative constructions. In this third section we shall also show that, independent of polarity concerns, monotonicity is pivotal to the semantics of gradable adjectives. In particular, we show that Van Benthem's theory of comparatives rests on monotonicity. In the fourth section we look at affective predicates with regard to comparative constructions. This section will lead us to the formulation of a list of goals that the semantics of affective predicates must seek to achieve. In the last section we use Van Benthem's theory of comparatives to formalise our semantic intuitions concerning the monotonic behaviour of (gradable) affective predicates. At this stage our story will have been told.

Now, the best way to close this introduction is by reminding the reader, although in an idealised fashion, of the main features of Ladusaw's account:

At first it was thought that licensing could be reduced to negation, that is, overt negation or a negative feature built up in the syntactic derivational history of sentences. Then it was noticed that there are several natural language expressions that satisfy patterns of inference commonly seen as typical of negation. Let us examine this matter a little further. Negation in classical propositional logic shows the following property, the *Modus Tollendo Tollens* of Medieval Logic:[1]

(3)

$$\frac{\neg B \quad A \to B}{\neg A}$$

The interesting thing now is that several sentence operators that Klima identified as polarity triggers display this logical pattern. For instance, the adverb *rarely* does:

(4)

$$\frac{\text{Abelard rarely eats fruit} \quad \text{Abelard eats mangos} \to \text{he eats fruit}}{\text{Abelard rarely eats mangos}}$$

It seems, therefore, that expressions collected together only in virtue of their ability to trigger negative polarity items have, after all, another property: they satisfy the *Tollendo Tollens* pattern of inference. But we can go a step further and Ladusaw in fact did. He noticed that several non-sentential triggers display this same pattern of negation. For instance, the determiner *every* licenses polarity items in the first position, witness the sentence *Every man who has any child will understand.* The inferential pattern, on the other hand, is illustrated below:

(5)

$$\frac{\text{Every } CN_1 \text{ VP} \quad CN_2 \subseteq CN_1}{\text{Every } CN_2 \text{ VP}}$$

Note that both (3) and (5) contain a premise that expresses a relation between the (denotations of) expressions involved in the inference. However, while in the sentential case the relevant relation is that of implication, in the other one the relation is that of inclusion. Any expression that exemplifies the *Tollendo Tollens* pattern, be it at sentential level or below it, is called *downward monotone.* Before formulating the licensing hypothesis put forward by Ladusaw, we need a general characterisation of the relevant notion of monotonicity. To say that the context *C[X]*

---

[1]Fauconnier 1978 speaks of *implication reversal* taking *contraposition* as salient property of negation, i.e. the pattern: $A \to B \models \neg B \to \neg A$.

is downward monotone in the constituent X boils down to the validity of the pattern:

(6)
$$\frac{C[X] \quad Y \sqsubseteq X}{C[Y]}$$

Thus it can be said that the determiner *every* and the adverb *rarely* are downward monotone expressions. It is in terms of this definition of downward monotonicity that we shall formulate Ladusaw's Hypothesis.

Ladusaw's Licensing Hypothesis The sentence C[npi] is grammatical if and only if C[X] is downward monotone in X.

We have now given a rough description of the semantic account of polarity developed by Ladusaw. To illustrate some of the open problems facing Ladusaw's Hypothesis we turn now to the relationship between this hypothesis and affective predicates. It is worth remembering that the generally accepted view is that Ladusaw's Hypothesis comes to grief on the face of these predicates. That this is a reasonable complaint will be argued in the next paragraphs.

2   Ladusaw's Hypothesis and Affective Predicates

To put the matter in perspective, note that in (6) the generalised notion of implication, $\sqsubseteq$, is not fully interpreted. In its pristine form it stands for a general notion of *implication order* on arbitrary denotations.[2] Let us suppose that this order can take only two values: either set inclusion or material implication. We shall argue that both of them are inadequate when affective predicates come to the fore.

Affective Predicates and Set Inclusion

In the first place, brief reflection shows that in applying Ladusaw's Hypothesis to predicates the implication order cannot be simple Boolean inclusion. The following invalid inference shows why:

(7)
$$\frac{\text{It is odd that the author of } \textit{Small is beautiful} \text{ bought a car} \quad \text{small car} \subset \text{car}}{\text{It is odd that the author of } \textit{Small is beautiful} \text{ bought a small car}}$$

---

[2]This abstract representation of a general implication is elaborated in van Benthem 1986.

The point is that we can be surprised by the fact that our author bought a car, but knowing what we know about him we do not need to be surprised by his choice of a small one.

Affective Predicates and Material Implication

In the second place, material implication is also inadequate. Note first that some affective predicates seem to imply the embedded clause. They are what we call *veridical* sentence operators. So it seems that the following inference is valid:

(8)

$$\frac{\text{It is is amazing that Abelard bought a car}}{\text{Abelard bought a car}}$$

With regard to these affective predicates one must conclude that the implication order involved cannot be induced by material implication. The following argument shows why:

(9)

$$\frac{\text{It is amazing that } A \quad A \wedge \neg A \to A}{\frac{\text{It is amazing that } A \wedge \neg A}{A \wedge \neg A}}$$

But it is clear that it would not speak well for Ladusaw's Hypothesis if it forced us to accept that a contradiction follows from the use of the predicate *amazing*.

It has been suggested that the problem of veridical affective predicates can be resolved by restricting attention to those situations in which the embedded clause of the conclusion holds.[3] I shall use this suggestion in my own proposal; but as long as the implication order is material implication, this restriction is not strong enough. The following derivation shows that without further constraints any true proposition q would turn out to be an amazing one:

(10)

$$\frac{\frac{\text{It is amazing that } A}{A} \quad B \to A \quad \text{It is amazing that } A}{\text{It is amazing that } B}$$

---

[3] In Linebarger 1980 the author says that this is a move proposed to her by Ladusaw himself.

But this state of affairs is an unpalatable one. So, let us consider where we stand. The discussion so far shows that interpreting the implication order of (6) in the obvious ways does not support Ladusaw's Hypothesis. In fact, the relation between veridicality and downward monotonicity seems to falsify it.

So much then for ways in which affective predicates are problematic for Ladusaw's account. It appears to me, however, that these problems should not be considered to be bigger than they really are. What has been established is that affective predicates do not satisfy the pattern displayed in (6) when the implication order is interpreted as set inclusion or sentential implication. But it has not been shown that all sensible ways of validating that downward pattern of inference will lead to the defeat of Ladusaw's Hypothesis. In fact, as pointed out before, I would like to argue that the polarity behaviour of affective predicates is in harmony with Ladusaw's Hypothesis. This point will be the subject of later sections. First, as an initial step towards our final proposal, we shall consider a broad notion of monotonicity in the context of comparative constructions.

3 Comparatives and Monotonicity

Upon reflection on the monotonicity pattern (6) it is impossible not to notice the following feature. In order to make use of this pattern, it is necessary to have at our disposal a denotation domain with an implication order on it. In the case of sentential triggers , the domain is a set of truth values and the ordering is material implication. In the case of the determiners, the domain is a set of sets and the ordering relation is inclusion. The abstract form of this ordered denotation domain is then

$$(\mathbf{D}, \mathbf{R})$$

where $\mathbf{R}$ is an implication order of $\mathbf{D}$.

In this section it will be shown that the exclusive attention to sentential implication and set inclusion is an unfair one. It is fairly easily overlooked that expressions can be monotone along other perspectives than the Boolean ones. In particular we argue that gradable adjectives exemplify monotonicity patterns along the perspective provided by comparative constructions: the ordering induced by the comparatives can be identified with the implication order that monotonicity requires.

So, let A, B be gradable opposite adjectives, $\mathbf{D}$ the union of their denotations, and, finally, let $>_A$ be the binary relation that corresponds to the comparative form of A. We claim that, for the cases in which we are interested

$$(\mathbf{D}, >_A)$$

is an adequate background model for monotonicity.

I think that this is a fair guess: it is uncontroversial that the comparative form of a predicate orders the extension of the predicate itself. We can even take one step further and say that it is only reasonable to expect that the semantics of adjectives and comparatives validates the upward monotone pattern that we present here below:

(11)

$$\frac{\text{x is A} \quad \text{y} >_A \text{x}}{\text{y is A}}$$

This schema seems to be valid and it is inviting to develop semantic theories of comparatives that bear out this validity. And as a matter of fact, the type of monotonicity exemplified in the above pattern belongs to the core of modern treatments of comparatives. For instance, in Fauconnier 1978 this pattern of upward monotonicity is called the *Scale Principle*:

A scale of elements $(x_1, x_2, \ldots)$ is associated pragmatically with a propositional schema $R(X)$ if it is assumed that for any two elements on the scale, x_1 and x_2, x_2 higher than x_1, $R(x_1)$ entails $R(x_2)$.

Perhaps more significant is the fact that upward monotonicity turns out to be fully equivalent to one of the principles on which Van Benthem bases his theory of comparison. For the further development of this paper, it will be rewarding to spell out, in some detail, the way in which one can reveal monotonicity at the bottom of Van Benthem's comparison theory.

Van Benthem's Theory of Comparatives

In van Benthem 1983 we find a theory of comparatives that starts off from the observation that their adjectival base is context-dependent. Thus Abelard can be a tall European while he is a short Dutchman. Here, the reference group is responsible for the difference. In the first case the reference group consists of the people from Europe, in the second case it consists only of the people from the Netherlands. Now for comparatives Van Benthem introduces the following definition and principles:

Let A be any gradable adjective. Then

Definition 1 Heloise is more A than Abelard *means* There is a context c in which Heloise is A while Abelard is not.

Definition 2 [No Reversal] If there is a context c in which x is A, while y is not, then for all contexts c' that contain x it holds that if y is A in c' then so is x.

Definition 3 [Upward Difference] If there is a context c in which x is A, while y is not, then for all contexts c' $\supseteq$ c it holds that some z is A in c' while some v is not.

Definition 4 [Downward Difference] If there is a context c in which x is A, while y is not, then for all contexts c' such that $\{x, y\} \subseteq c'$ $\subseteq$ c it holds that in c' some z is A while some v is not.

On the basis of the above definition and principles Van Benthem proves, among other things, that comparatives are an almost-connected strict partial ordering: they are almost-connected, transitive and ir-reflexive. In a later section we shall adapt those principles to our own purposes. In the meantime we want to introduce this definition:

Definition 5 [Upward Monotonicity] A is upward monotone if for any context c that contains y, in which x is A, while y is more A that x, holds that y is A as well.

The central position of monotonicity can be gathered from the following proposition:

Proposition 1 *Upward Monotonicity and No Reversal are equivalent.*

Proof. Assume Monotonicity. Let c be a context in which y is A while x is not. Moreover, let c' be a context such that it both contains y and x is A in it. Now, by our first definition it follows that in c', y is more A than x. But then, by monotonicity, we establish that y is A in c'. Thus No Reversal holds.

Assume now No Reversal. Let c be any context that contains y, in which it is true that x is A and in which it is true that y is more A than x. By Definition 1, there is a context c' in which y is A while x is not. But this information sets No Reversal in movement. Since c satisfies the description of the universal clause of No Reversal, we conclude that y is A in c. Thus, upward monotonicity holds. □

Let me point out that Klein 1980 uses principles similar to the first two of Van Benthem. We will not explore this possibility here but it seems a safe guess that the previous result can be extended to Klein's theory as well.

The following proposition has important empirical consequences:

Proposition 2 *The set $\{x$ is A, y is more A than $x\}$ is not satisfiable in a structure with exactly two elements that satisfies Upward Monotonicity and Upward Difference.*

Proof. Suppose that in the context c $= \{x, y\}$ it holds both that x is

A and that y is more A than x. Then, by Monotonicity we conclude that y is also A in c. This means, of course, that the complement of A in c is empty. However, by definition, there is a context in which y is A while x is not. This information activates Upward Difference thus entailing that the complement of A in c must be non-empty. A contradiction. □

Remember that my concern is not only upward monotonicity but also its downward counterpart. We shall presently turn back to the affective predicates but first I shall take into account their interplay with comparative constructions.

4 Affective Predicates as Monotone Expressions

We take as a starting point some obvious facts about affective predicates. It is especially notable that a great number of these expressions

- are gradable predicates
- form opposite pairs with non-affective predicates
- can be combined in downward inferences with the comparative form of the opposite

An illustration will clarify these points. Consider the affective predicate *stupid*, and its opposite *smart*. First, note that *more stupid* is a felicitous piece of English and that so is *more smart*. Secondly, it is also clear that these two adjectives form a pair of opposites: to say of an object that it is smart commits one to the assertion that it is not stupid; and to say of an object that it is stupid conveys the assertion that it is not smart. Moreover, that *smart* is not an affective predicate is shown by the anomalous sentence below:

(12) He was smart to become any heavier.

Lastly, the third feature of affective predicates is illustrated here below:

(13)

$$\frac{\text{Abelard is stupid} \quad \text{Abelard} >_{smart} \text{Heloise}}{\text{Heloise is stupid}}$$

This inference gives the clue to what is meant by saying that the affective *stupid* is downward monotone. An intuitive explanation of its validity may be this. Since Abelard is smarter than Heloise, in the ordering induced by this comparative Heloise ranks lower than Abelard. But to say that Abelard is stupid is to say that he ranks pretty low in the ordering of smartness. So Heloise must also belong to the lower part of the smartness ordering since she has a position even lower than the position of the low placed Abelard. But this is exactly what the downward monotonicity pattern leads us to expect.

We shall try to make all this more precise in a later section. For the time being let us add that there are numerous pairs of predicates that behave as the pair (stupid; smart) does in the previous inference. Consider, for instance, the inferential behaviour of the pairs of predicates (likely; unlikely) (surprising; expected):

(14)

$$\frac{\text{That he goes is unlikely} \quad \text{That he goes} >_{likely} \text{that she goes}}{\text{That she goes is unlikely}}$$

(15)

$$\frac{\text{That he went is surprising} \quad \text{That he went} >_{expected} \text{that she went}}{\text{That she went is surprising}}$$

Now we must remember the caveat we mentioned at an earlier stage: *Surprising* is a veridical predicate in that it demands the truth of its subordinate clause. For instance it could very well be the case both that p is surprising and that p is more expected than q. But if q fails to be true, then it will be strange to claim that q is surprising. To get around this difficulty we follow Ladusaw's advice and restrict our attention to those cases in which q is given. This move, of course, has no affect on the monotonicity pattern itself beyond reducing it to local contexts satisfying an additional condition. Observe also that it is not possible to set up arguments similar to (9) and (10) because the underlying ordering is no longer an ordering of truth-values.

The drift of this section is the claim that the affective predicate B satisfies the downward pattern, where (A, B) is a pair of opposite predicates:

(16)

$$\frac{\text{x is B} \quad \text{x} >_A \text{y}}{\text{y is B}}$$

So, in order to explain that a certain gradable affective predicates B license polarity items we associate it with a semantics that enforces the validity of the above downward pattern of inference. If this association is non arbitrary, then we shall have proven Ladusaw's point: licensers are downward operators.

It may however be objected that, besides the affective predicates, there must be other predicates that satisfy (16), namely their opposites. I shall not dispute this point but I shall try to diminish its significance. For in a later part of this paper I shall undertake to try to produce a semantics in which the opposite of an affective predicate validates our downward pattern *vacuously*. To understand this move it will be helpful to keep in mind that monotonicity does not exhaust the semantics of affective predicates and their opposites. Another important feature, shared with non-affective predicates, concerns marking and neutrality. We shall concentrate our attention to affective predicates that behave rather like *shorter* than like *taller* in the following passage in Johnson-Laird 1993:

> *taller than* is a neutral expression that implies nothing about the absolute heights of the entities it relates, whereas *shorter than* suggests that these entities are short rather than tall.

In the next section I argue that due to its marked character the opposites of affective predicates fail to satisfy (16) in a substantive way. On the positive side, we shall also see that marking offers an independent characterisation of a large number of affective predicates.

5 Goals for the Semantics of Opposites

Let us first approach these matters by asking a quite natural question. Which assumptions about comparatives can be used to explain the validity of the inferences (13–15) presented in the previous section? The first that comes to mind is assumption that comparatives of opposite predicates are converse relations. We may tentatively assume that for any pair of opposite predicates (A, B) holds that $y >_A x$ implies $x >_B y$. Then the examples of the previous section could be reduced to the upward pattern since we can set up inferences of the following kind:

(17)

$$\frac{\text{Abelard} >_{smart} \text{Heloise}}{\text{Abelard is stupid} \quad \frac{\text{Heloise} >_{stupid} \text{Abelard}}{\text{Heloise is stupid}}}$$

Since upward monotonicity is widely accepted this could be the right way of approaching the matter. But there is at least one doubtful step in the above inference: Is it at all reasonable that comparatives of opposite predicates are converse relations? The insight that not all pairs of opposites are converse relations goes back to Sapir 1944. Although *stupid* and *smart* are clearly opposites we fight shy of ordering smart people according to their stupidity. On the contrary, there is a strong intuition according to which if Heloise is smart it is inappropriate to state *Heloise is more stupid than Abelard*. Conversely, if it is true that Heloise is more stupid than Abelard, we hesitate to say that Heloise is smart. Therefore, there will be something odd in reducing the validity of the downward pattern of inference to the widely accepted pattern of upward monotonicity supplemented with the conversion assumption.

In this paper we develop a semantics that explains the validity of the inferences (13–15) without resorting to the assumption that the opposites produce converse relations. We incorporate, instead, the assumption that the comparative of an affective predicate orders the extension of this predicate only. This means that if it is true that x is more B than y we can safely conclude that x is not A. Of course, this situation is compatible with x being B. However, adopt here the weakest possibility: x is more B than y will entail that x belongs to the complement of A.

Thus, in our semantics we shall say that *more stupid* is essentially marked, that is, from *Abelard is more stupid than Heloise* we conclude that he is not smart. A similar entailment will not be made available for the construction *Abelard is more smart than Heloise*. It is evident that this semantics attributes the uneasiness we experience with the inference *x is more smart than y*, ergo *y is more stupid than x* to the fact that the marked predicate has more content than its neutral counterpart.

It is worth remarking, before we address the formal implementation of our intuitions, that there is a variance with regard to the acceptability of inferences like the previous one (cf. Åqvist 1981). The fact that there is no universal rejection of this inference is reflected in our semantics by the fact that any counter-example to the above inference demands models of at least three elements. As long as we limit the contexts of comparison to the two objects explicitly mentioned in a comparison, there is no way for us to invalidate the converse assumption. But the reader must try to keep in mind that in the original architecture of our comparative semantics, structures with exactly two elements fail to satisfy the set { x is A, y is more A than y}. This is namely the content of Proposition 2. But this means that if in such a model *y is more A than x* is true, then we can conclude that the sentence *x is A* cannot be true. Therefore, in such a model the sentences *x is more B than y* and *y is more A than x* have the same surplus of meaning. This is the reason why in our semantics the converse assumption is bore out by a context with only two elements. Thus, in our approach we go a long way in accommodating conflicting intuitions concerning the behaviour of marked comparatives and their neutral opposites.

In general, marked comparatives will correspond to marked adjectives. As is well known there are some intuitive tests that help us to determine, in concrete situations, whether a predicate is neutral or not. Thus, evidence of marking is offered by the fact that it is the neutral predicate that is used in non-committal questions, i.e., How smart is Abelard? will be the non-committal question against the loaded How stupid is Abelard. In general, it appears that affective predicates are not used in neutral questions. Thus the neutral questions are How pleasant was it? How sensible is it? How convenient is it? rather than How annoying was it? How absurd is it? How inconvenient is it? This suggest that in this paper we are dealing with affective predicates that have an extra property : they are marked predicates.

Let us pause briefly to assess the relevance of these observations for our enterprise. What becomes clear is this. In general, a degree predicate that is also an affective predicate is a marked one.[4] Moreover, its comparative will also be a marked predicate. Finally, the neutral opposite companion of an affective predicate provides the dimension along which this last predicate is downward monotone.

The considerations in this section yield several goals which an empirically adequate semantics of affective predicates must be seen to achieve. The semantics must

- make the comparative of gradable affective predicates marked
- warrant that all gradable predicates are upward monotone along the dimension of their own comparative
- warrant that the comparative of a marked predicate implies the comparative of its neutral opposite but not the other way around
- warrant that affective predicates are downward monotone with regard to the comparative of their opposite

To the achievement of these goals, the next section is devoted.

6 A Monotone Semantics for Comparatives

As we pointed out before, Van Benthem's theory of comparison will be the framework within we shall try to achieve our goals. However, the considerations presented in the previous sections require us to modify Van Benthem's theory a very little. In the first place we shall concentrate our attention on predicates that take clauses as arguments. This is due to the obvious reason that these predicates are the ones that license polarity items. Of course, other predicates will still be used for the sake of

---

[4]I said *in general* because I reluctantly have to thank H. Klein by pointing out that the licenser *difficult* is a neutral gradable adjective.

exposition. In the second place, we shall be dealing with pairs of opposite predicates.[5] The most natural way of doing this would be to identify the denotation of the opposite of predicate A with the complement of the denotation of A. This strategy is not attractive to us because we are aiming at a semantics faithful to the intuition that marked comparatives have an inferential behaviour different from that of neutral comparatives. We shall incorporate this difference into the definition of the marked comparatives. By so doing we are committing ourselves to show that the marked comparatives are still an almost connected strict partial ordering.

We have also decided to adopt a stronger version of *Downward Difference*. We shall say, for instance, that if in a context c you establish that x is big while y is not, then in the context consisting of only x and y, x is big while y is small. Thus we assume that differences between objects x, y that are expressed in terms of one member of an opposite pair A/B, (x is A while y is not A), will be expressed in terms of both opposites (x is A while y is B) whenever the context consists of exactly those two objects. This means that the comparative construction x *is more A than* y will have the meaning y *is B insofar as x is A* whenever we focus on the comparison set $\{x, y\}$. It should be observed that in the original formulation of the theory under consideration, this strong form of downward difference is proven to follow from Van Benthem's original principles.

Our proposal

Consider a pair of opposite gradable predicates A/B where A is the neutral member of the pair and both take clauses as arguments. We shall be discussing the semantics of sentences built up from these adjectives and a set of sentence letters: p_1, p_2, p_3, ... We reintroduce here the symbol $>_X$ used in the previous sections. The formulas we shall be concerned with are defined in the following way:

Definition 6   1. If p is a sentence letter, then $A(p)$, $B(p)$ are sentences.

2. If p, q are sentence letters, then $p >_A q$, $p >_B q$ are sentences.

Definition 7 A *comparative* model for A/B is a structure $(C, \mathbf{C}, \mathcal{F})$ where

1. C is a nonempty set of sentences
2. $\mathbf{C}$ is the collection of finite subsets of C.

---

[5] Van Benthem himself points out that in pushing his analysis a little further along linguistic lines one must introduce *opposite pairs* such as tall/short.

3. $\mathcal{F}$ is a binary function such that for each $c \in \mathbf{C}$, $\mathcal{F}(A, c)$, $\mathcal{F}(B, c)$ are disjoint subsets of c.

We denote $\mathcal{F}(X, c)$ by X_c, where X stands for A or B.

Notice that the third clause allows us to conclude $p \notin A_c$ whenever $p \in B_c$.

Next we define the relation $\models$ between contexts and sentences. We adapt Van Benthem's definition to the special case of marked comparatives and make explicit the assumption that a comparative is meaningful in a context provided the elements that are being compared belong to it.

Definition 8

1. $c \models X(p)$ iff $p \in X_c$
2. $c \models p >_A q$ iff
   - $p, q \in c$
   - $\exists c' \in \mathbf{C}$ such that $\{p, q\} \subseteq c'$, $c' \models A(p)$ and $c' \not\models A(q)$.
3. $c \models p >_B q$ iff
   - $p, q \in c$
   - $\exists c' \in \mathbf{C}$ such that $\{p, q\} \subseteq c'$, $c' \models B(p)$ and $c' \not\models B(q)$, and
   - $c \not\models A(p)$.

Notice that clause (1) warrants that p is in c whenever $p \in X_c$ since $X_c \subseteq c$.

Definition 9 [No Reversal]

A comparative model will be called *No Reversal* if it satisfies the condition:

If there is a $c \in C$ such that $\{p, q\} \subseteq c$, $c \models A(p)$ and $c \not\models A(q)$, or $c \models B(q)$ and $c \not\models B(p)$ then for all $c' \in \mathbf{C}$

1. If $p \in c'$ and $c' \models A(q)$ then $c' \models A(p)$
2. If $q \in c'$ and $c' \models B(p)$ then $c' \models B(q)$

A No Reversal model is called *Faithful* if it satisfies the following difference conditions:

Definition 10 [Upward Difference]

If there is a $c \in C$ such that $c \models A(p)$ and $c \models B(q)$, then for all $c' \supseteq c$ holds that neither $A_{c'}$ nor $B_{c'}$ is empty.

Definition 11 [Strong Downward Difference]

If there is a $c \in C$ that contains both p and q but that is such that $c \models A(p)$ and $c \not\models A(q)$ or $\models B(q)$ and $c \not\models B(p)$, then $\{p, q\} \models A(p)$ and $\{p, q\} \models B(q)$.

Now we are in a position to define a notion of logical consequence between sets of formulae Γ and single ones.

Definition 12 [Logical consequence]

$\Gamma \models_{\mathbf{C}} \phi$ iff

1. There is a No Reversal model $\mathbf{C'}$ and a $c' \in \mathbf{C'}$ such that $c' \models \Gamma$

2. $\forall c \in \mathbf{C}$ such that $c \models \Gamma$ it holds that $c \models \phi$.

The No Reversal Model and the Desiderata

Now we turn to the desiderata laid down in the previous section and we show that the semantics developed in this section actually helps us to achieve our goals.

Proposition 3 (Upward Monotonicity)

$A(q), p >_A q \models_{\mathbf{C}} A(p)$

Proof. Let c be any context such that $c \models A(q)$ and $c \models p >_A q$. The second premise implies that there is a context c' such that $c' \models A(p)$ and $c' \not\models A(q)$. Since $\{p, q\} \subseteq c'$ follows from the definition of the comparative, we can apply No Reversal. Now, we assumed that $c \models A(q)$. By definition, $p \in c$ also follows. Therefore $c \models A(p)$. $\square$

Proposition 4 (Upward Monotonicity)

$B(q), p >_B q \models_{\mathbf{C}} B(p)$

Proof. See previous proof. $\square$

Proposition 5 (Downward Monotonicity)

$B(p), p >_A q \models_{\mathbf{C}} B(q)$

Proof. The same proof as for Proposition (3), but now we use the other clause in the definition of No Reversal. $\square$

Proposition 6 (Vacuous Monotonicity)

$A(p), p >_B q \models_{\mathbf{C}} A(q)$

Proof. Note that the premises cannot be simultaneously satisfied: Any context that satisfies $p >_B q$ fails to satisfy $A(p)$. But this contradicts the other premise. So, vacuously, any context in a No Reversal model verifies Downward Monotonicity for neutral predicates. $\square$

Proposition 7 (That opposite comparatives are partially converse ...)

$p >_B q \models q >_A p$

Proof. Let c be any context in which $p >_B q$ holds. Then $p, q \in c$ and there is a context c' than contains p and q such that $c' \models B(p)$

and c' $\not\models$ B(q). By Downward Difference we conclude $\{p, q\} \models$ B(p) and $\{p, q\} \models$ A(q). Since in all contexts the denotations of A and B are disjunct we have $\{p, q\} \not\models$ A(p). Therefore, we conclude: $q >_A p$ holds in c. □

Proposition 8 (but not fully converse)
$$p >_A q \models q \not>_B p$$

Proof. The point is that we allow the possibility of having a context c with $c \models p >_A q$ and $c \models$ A(q). Although it follows that there is a context in which q is B and p is not we cannot conclude that $q >_B p$ because of q being A in c. □

Proposition 9 *In a two elements model the entailment* $p >_A q \models q >_B p$ *holds.*

Proof. Let $c = \{p, q\}$. By a by now familiar argument the premise allows us to assert that in c p is A and q is B. A fortiori, the conclusion is also true in this model. □

It is worthwhile to note that in two element models the propositions concerning monotonicity are validated vacuously.

Finally we want to show that in a Faithful model Strong Downward Difference is equivalent to the following condition:

Definition 13 [Downward Difference]
If there is a context c in which p is A while q is not, or in which q is B while p is not, then in any context $c' \subseteq c$ that contains p and q neither $A_{c'}$ nor $B_{c'}$ is empty.

Proposition 10 *In a faithful model Strong Downward Difference is equivalent to Downward Difference.*

Proof. Suppose there is a context c in which the sentence p is A while the sentence q is not or in which q is B while p is not.
Now, Strong Downward Difference implies that in the context $\{p, q\}$, the sentence p will be A while q will be B. Therefore, by Upward Difference, it holds for any $c' \supseteq \{p, q\}$ that neither $A_{c'}$ nor $B_{c'}$ is empty. A fortiori in no subset of c containing p and q will any of those sets be empty.
On the other hand Downward Difference implies that in the context $\{p, q\}$, A nor B are empty. But now, by No Reversal, we may conclude that in this context p is A while q is B. For if p is B then so is q. But this means that in $\{p, q\}$, the predicate A will be empty. Therefore, in this context p cannot be B and since something must be in this set, it has to be q. But this means that p has to be A. □

Relational properties of marked comparatives

Before closing this section we should address a question that the reader may already have framed: Do marked comparatives still have the familiar properties of comparatives? Notice that by definition any marked comparative is irreflexive. Now we show that Van Benthem's proofs of transitivity and almost-connectedness carry over to marked comparatives.

Proposition 11 (Transitivity)
$$p >_B q, \ q >_B r \models_{\mathbf{C}} p >_B r.$$

Proof. Let c be such that $c \models p >_B q$, $c \models q >_B r$. By definition the first premise yields that $c \not\models A(p)$ and in combination with the second one it warrants that the set $c' = \{p, q, r\}$ is a subset of c. Moreover, the first premise also yields a context c" in which p is B while q is not. By Downward Difference this means that in $\{p, q\}$, p is B while q is A. Therefore, by Upward Difference, we know that neither $A_{c'}$ nor $B_{c'}$ is empty.

Suppose then that $r \in B_{c'}$. No Reversal forces us to conclude that both q and p are in $B_{c'}$. But this contradicts the non emptiness of $A_{c'}$. Hence $r \notin B_{c'}$. Therefore p or q are the only possible members of $B_{c'}$. But by No Reversal if q is in this set so is p. Thus we can be sure that p is in $B_{c'}$ and therefore that $c' \models B(p)$ holds.

Consider now the elements of $A_{c'}$. Given that p is in $B_{c'}$, the only possible members of $A_{c'}$ are q and r. But if $q \in A_{c'}$ then, by No Reversal, $r \in A_{c'}$. Thus we know for sure that $r \in A_{c'}$. But this implies $c' \not\models B(r)$.

   Now we conclude $c \models p >_B r$ since there is a context, namely c', that contains both p and r and in which p is B while r is not. Moreover c itself contains p and r and in this context p isn't A. □

Proposition 12 (Almost-connectedness)
   If $c \models p >_B q$, then $c \models p >_B r$ or $c \models r >_B q$ for all r in the set B_c.

Proof. Let $c \models p >_B q$. Notice that in c the sentence p will not be A. Consider the context $c' = \{p, q, r\}$ where r is a member of B_c. As in the previous proof we argue that in the context c' both $A_{c'}$ and $B_{c'}$ are nonempty. Consider now r against this background.

Suppose it is A in c'. As in the previous proof we infer that p must be B in this context. Moreover r cannot be B here. Therefore, in c, $p >_B r$ will hold, since p isn't A in the context c.

Suppose r is B in c'. Then, as previously, we infer that q must be A in this context. But then q is not B therein. Now, since by assumption r belongs to the set B_c we are allowed to conclude $r >_B q$.

Suppose r is neither B nor A in c'. In this case there are two possibilities:

1. p is A while q is B
2. p is B while q is A

But notice that if p is A then, by No Reversal, q will also be A, thus contradicting the nonemptiness of $B_{c'}$. Therefore only the second possibility will count. But then, in fact, we are finished because this means that p is B in c'. Since in this context q is not B while in the original context c, that contains both p and q, we had that p is B, we conclude that $c \models p >_B q$ holds. □

Now we have reached the point in which the semantics put forward in this section is seen to satisfy the desiderata we imposed upon it:

- The comparative of gradable affective predicates is marked
- The comparative of an affective predicate entails the comparative of its opposite but not vice versa
- Gradable predicates are upward monotone along the dimension of their own comparative
- Affective predicates are downward monotone with regard to the comparative of their opposite
- The neutral polar companion of an affective predicate is vacuously downward
- The marked comparatives have the familiar relational properties

Veridical Affective Predicates

There is still a problem we have to confront. We have pointed out that there is a widespread belief in the existence of veridical predicates. To accomodate inferences involving such expressions our semantics has to be augmented. This is done in the following way. With each $c \in \mathbf{C}$ we associate one of its subsets: the set of sentences that holds at c. This subset will be denoted by **c**. A veridical predicate X is characterized by the fact that $X_c \subseteq \mathbf{c}$. Then we extend definition (8) with the clause:

$$c \models p \text{ iff } p \in \mathbf{c}.$$

It should be clear that monotone inferences involving veridical affective predicates will hold only in contexts in which the embedded clause of the conclusion holds. Because if we infer that $X(p)$ holds in c while this sentence is not a member of c, it will follow that in this context p is not in X_c. This is the content of Ladusaw's advice to Linebarger and the semantics presented here is its natural context.

7 Final Words

We have established in this paper that by taking affective predicates as gradable predicates one can prove that they are downward monotone. This move forces us to interpret the comparatives as the relevant notion of implication in the definition of monotonicity. It is important to keep in mind that the ordering induced by comparatives is a natural one; the reason being that there is a intimate connection between the meaning of the predicate and the ordering. So, we did not need to postulate the existence of an implication order whose only justification is to avoid the shipwreck of our favorite theory on polarity. That comparatives are orderings and that they order the denotation of adjectives are strong, almost theory free intuitions. Moreover, in formal semantics there is a consensus concerning the relation of adjectives and their comparatives: their meanings are closely intertwined. Therefore, comparatives can be used as an interpretation of the implication order needed in the characterization of monotonicity. That in practice this view is fruitful has been argued in the previous pages.

References

Åqvist, L. 1981. Predicate Calculi with Adjectives and Nouns. *Journal of Philosophy of Logic* 10(1):1–26.

Bach, E. 1989. *Informal Lectures on Formal Semantics*. State University of New York Press.

Baker, C.L. 1970. Double Negatives. *Linguistic Inquiry* 1:169–186.

van Benthem, Johan. 1983. *The Logic of Time*. Dordrecht: Reidel.

van Benthem, Johan. 1986. *Essays in Logical Semantics*. Dordrecht: Reidel.

Fauconnier, Gilles. 1975. Polarity and the Scale Principle. In *CLS 11*. 188–199. Chicago: Chicago Linguistic Society.

Fauconnier, Gilles. 1978. Implication Reversal in a Natural Language. In *Formal Semantics and Pragmatics for Natural Languages*, ed. F. Guenther and S.J. Schmidt. 289–301. Dordrecht: Reidel.

Johnson-Laird, P.N. 1993. *Mental Models*. Cambridge, Mass: Harvard University Press.

Klein, E. 1980. A Semantics for Positive and Comparative Adjectives. *Linguistics and Philosophy* 89:1–45.

Klima, E. S. 1964. Negation in English. In *Formal Methods in the Study of Language*, ed. J.A. Fodor and J. Katz. 246–323. Englewood Cliffs: Prentice Hall.

Ladusaw, William A. 1979. *Polarity Sensitivity as Inherent Scope Relations.* Doctoral dissertation, University of Texas at Austin. Distributed by IULC, Bloomington, Indiana, 1980.

Linebarger, Marcia. 1980. *The Grammar of Negative Polarity.* Doctoral dissertation, MIT. Distributed by IULC, Bloomington, Indiana, 1981.

Progovac, Ljiljana. 1994. *Negative and Positive Polarity. A Binding Approach.* Cambridge: Cambridge University Press.

Sapir, E. 1944. Grading: A Study in Semantics. *Philosophy of Science* 11:93–116.

6

HPSG as Type Theory

M. ANDREW MOSHIER

1 Introduction

Formal grammar has enjoyed a long connection to the mathematical field of type theory. Indeed, Categorial Grammar, henceforth CG, (Lambek 1961) , can nearly be summed up by the slogan "Grammar is Type Theory." In a less overt way, Generalized Phrase Structure Grammar (Gazdar *et al.* 1985) is concerned with getting at a notion of syntactic type (or category). As successor to GPSG, Head-driven Phrase Structure Grammar, henceforth HPSG, (Pollard and Sag 1994) likewise takes the assignment of a sort (or type) of feature structure to a linguistic sign as a fundamental task. Other connections to type theory have recently found their way into Lexical Function Grammar (Dalrymple *et al.* 1995) as well (particularly, as related to linear logic). Nevertheless, there are substantial differences in the way that CG versus HPSG treats types. In CG, the metamathematics of type theory is a significant emphasis; much of the CG program is to do with the details of the underlying type theory: does it have products, exponents? is composition available for functional types, or only application? Much of the type theory of CG, then, concerns combinatorial mechanisms. In contrast, the type theory of HPSG is impoverished; it has almost no mechanisms for constructing new types. Except for appeal to specific schematic definitions such "list-of" types, HPSG treats each type (called a "sort" in that theory) as basic from the perpective of type theory. One of the great values of viewing a system of formal grammar as type theory — witnessed, for example, in the book by Morrill 1994 on recent developments in CG — is that it establishes a route for transfer of results. Similar transfers of results came much earlier in, e.g., van Benthem 1983, and in Keenan and Faltz 1985 (the latter not being overtly type-thoeretic, but still informed

Computing Natural Language.
Atocha Aliseda, Rob van Glabbeek, and Dag Westerståhl, editors.
Copyright © 1998, Stanford University.

by similar ideas). To a smaller extent, this is also witnessed in HPSG in Carpenter 1993, and in King 1989, but because of the impoverished use of type theory *qua* type theory in HSPG, such transfer has been quite limited. The main task of this paper is to enrich the type theory of HPSG and to demonstrate that the result yields explanations of important theory-internal concepts, in particular, the concepts of "feature" and of "principle".

One of the central activities in the development of HPSG is the argument about placement of features within the feature geometry of signs. Another is, of course, the argument about what principles are at work. The two go on simultaneously and often in concert. Nevertheless it makes some sense, for example, to separate the argument to do with the precise location of the HEAD feature from the argument to do with the Head Feature Principle. In fact, to look at current HPSG formalisms, it appears that placement of features comes first while statement of principles comes second. That is, the principles are stated formally with reference to specific appropriateness conditions, which have to do mainly with placement of features. In Moshier 1997a and 1997b, I have argued that this order is backward if we take seriously the notion that an important methodological advantage of HPSG is that predictions can be infered from the interaction of independent principles. In this paper, I argue that it is backward for another reason: the principles of HPSG *determine* feature geometry and not the other way around. Following that argument, I propose an alternative type-theoretic framework for HPSG, in which a principle can be stated as a definition that determines all parts of the feature geometry having to do with a particular linguistic phenomenon. The feature logic of HPSG is an impoverished type theory — one having no type constructors (all types are basic), one morphism constructor (concatenation of paths amounts to composition) and one constraint on the interpretation of types (the "sort hierarchy" allows a grammarian to insist that one type be understood as a disjoint union of other types). So what I propose here is essentially to enrich feature logic to make it a full-fledged type theory. Importantly, the type theory provides a means to formalize, not only an HPSG principle as it is currently formalized, but also to specify a principle's precise role in the linguistic theory and specifically in arguments about feature placement.

The notion that principles determine feature geometry is already present in the HPSG literature. For example, in Pollard and Sag 1994 (16-21), Pollard and Sag argue that CATEGORY is appropriate for the sort *local* precisely because (i) the *local* characteristics of a sign are those that can be shared between a trace and its filler in an unbounded dependency (this is part of the Head Filler Schema of the ID Principle) and (ii) the category (traditional part of speech plus subcategorization characteristics) of a sign is one characteristic that can be so shared. In other words, the Head Filler Schema requires that CATEGORY be appropriate for *local* on the strength of an *informal* understanding of the role that *local* plays and on an observation about categories. Similarly, the reason that LOCAL is appropropriate for *synsem* is simply that SYNSEM is supposed to yield precisely those characteristics of signs that can figure in selectional restrictions, and local characteristics (those shared between trace and filler) can figure in selectional restrictions. Similar arguments are nearly ubiquituous in the HPSG literature. Consider the arguments in Netter 1994 about functional heads and the feature geometry needed to explain a number of agreement facts in German and in Oliva 1992 or Calcagno 1993, about word order. These papers argue largely about the details of feature geometry, and those arguments hinge on informal understandings as to what various sorts and features mean in the theory.

Put the other way, in the absence of the Subcategorization Principle, the LOCAL feature might as well be appropriate for *sign*. But in light of the special role that SYNSEM is supposed to play, we seem to have no choice in where LOCAL appears in the representation of a sign: it must appear "downstream" of SYNSEM. But in fact, nothing in the feature-based formalism of HPSG requires this because there is no mechanism for enforcing the special theoretical roles of SYNSEM, or HEAD or LOCAL. To see this, consider a version of HPSG in which the features LOCAL and HEAD are appropriate for *sign*. Then a Head Filler Schema would require that both the LOCAL and HEAD features be shared between a trace and its filler. Similarly, a Subcategorization Principle would involve two (or more) features SUBCAT-1 and SUBCAT-2 the values of which would be lists of *head* and lists of *local*. What is now a single identity condition would have to be two distinct, but formally very similar, identity conditions. Apart from the inelegence of such a theory, there is nothing really wrong with multiple versions of a principle, each one codifying a similar sort of interaction between features. However, if we can take seriously (and I mean, formally) the special role of features like SYNSEM, LOCAL and HEAD then we may actually make a formal commitment to the special roles that features such as HEAD, SYNSEM and LOCAL play.

The formalism presented here differs from familiar "feature logic" approaches in several ways:

1. Types are not necessarily atomic. The theory allows the construction of types corresponding to products, coproducts and lists. Amongst other advantages, this eliminates the need to code lists and other constructions in appropriateness conditions.

2. Features are not necessarily atomic. Specifically, the theory includes feature constructors relating constructed types to one another. For example, this allows us to formalize features of more than one argument, features that are determined by cases, features representing functional dependencies and features defined by primative recursion on lists.

3. The traditional distinction between a "feature" and a "path" is eliminated. Features are taken to be closed under composition, as well as several other operations.

4. The standard HPSG notion of appropriateness conditions and sort hierarchy are replaced by a single notion of typed features, making it just as reasonable to speak of a feature which is "co-appropriate" for a particular type as to speak of a feature that is appropriate for a particular type. Informally, a feature is appropriate for a type σ if it takes its arguments from σ, and it is co-appropriate for a type τ if it yields values in τ.

5. Via the concept of a universal feature, the typical informal argumentation about feature geometry is replaced by formal specification. For example, the question of whether a particular feature ought to be appropriate for *synsem* objects is determined by a formal specification that SYNSEM and SUBCAT comprise a *universal* subcategorization diagram.

6. Individuals (for example, individual signs) do not play a special role in the formalism. An individual sign is simply a special kind of feature that is co-appropriate for *sign*. But questions that one might pose about individual signs are equally poseable about parametric signs, i.e., any features co-appropriate for *sign*.

7. Token identity is eliminated. The theory involves only one concept of equality for features. Features are interpreted as functions, more generally as arrows in a category. Equality of features means equality of interpretation. There is no need to introduce the complication of a graph theoretical identity (that is, token identity) as distinct from structural isomorphism. This is essentially because individuals have no special status.

Also, the type theory developed here differs from the CG type theories in that it does not have exponents, i.e., "implication" or "functional" types. In CG, categories such as S/NP
NP (the category of transitive verbs) are interpreted by types such as "function from NP's to functions from NP's to S's". Such higher-order types are central to CG. In HPSG, on the other hand, the combinatorial properties of signs, formalized by higher order categories in CG, are

formalized by other mechanisms, particularly by subcategorization lists. This suggests that exponents are less an issue for HPSG that are lists. The type theory reflects this by not having an exponental construction but instead having a list construction.

Section 2 sets out a simple type theory. In Section 3, I show how a grammar can be rendered in the type theory, and how the type theoretic view of HPSG offers an understanding of parsing and generation. In addition, I point out an interesting analogy between parsing and linguistic argumentation. In Section 4, I show how to formulate some HPSG principles in the type theory and introduce the concept of a universal diagram as the formal counterpart to informal statements about the roles of various features within a grammar. The result is that certain features, such as SYNSEM, LOCAL and HEAD, will determine parts of the feature geometry of signs based on linguistic arguments regarding how features must interact. The novel point here is that the type theoretic framework allows us to make precise the formal consequences of particular kinds of argumentation in HPSG about feature geometry.

In Section 5, I consider how a lexicon might be organized in the type-theoretic formalism. This section is speculative, but I think demonstrates the power of a type-theoretic framework to solve technical problems in the formalization of HPSG. Notably, the proposal I make for the lexicon solves the problem of the theoretical status of both lexical entries (here they are simply parametric signs) and lexical rules (they are simply maps from one lexical entry to another), by explaining how they can be viewed as total entities and yet involve underspecification of the kinds necessary to formalize generalizations.

Section 6 presents the formal type theory, and mentions without proof some of the proof-theoretic properties of the formalism.

2   The Type Theory

The type theory considered here centers on the use of types that correspond to products, co-products and lists. These notions suffice for the purposes of this paper. The reader may refer to Beeson 1985 for a thorough development of various type theories that are similar in spirit to the one considered here. To my knowledge no one has considered precisely a type theory only of products, co-products and lists, but no surprising technical developments arise from this choice of types.

The theory involves three kinds of assertions. These are

σ:**Type** (called a *type assertion*),
$f\colon \sigma \to \tau$ (called a feature assertion) and
$(f = g)\colon \sigma \to \tau$ (called an equality assertion)

These are subject to assumptions. So the general form of a judgement (the sort of expression that may said to be *derivable*) is $\Sigma \vdash \phi$ where Σ is a set of assumptions and ϕ is an assertion. Σ also consists of assertions of particular kinds to be discussed below.

Types are formed from a fixed vocabulary of basic type symbols together with operators and punctuation marks. Assertions of the form s:**Type** may appear in Σ whenever s is a basic type symbol. The judgement $\Sigma \vdash s$:**Type** is always derivable when s:**Type** occurs in Σ. Also, $\Sigma \vdash 1$:**Type** and $\Sigma \vdash 0$:**Type** are always derivable. These two types are intended to denote a terminal and an initial type, respectively. Furthermore, if $\Sigma \vdash \sigma$:**Type** and $\Sigma \vdash \tau$:**Type** are derivable, then so are the following

$$\Sigma \quad \vdash \quad \sigma \times \tau\text{:\textbf{Type}}$$
$$\Sigma \quad \vdash \quad \sigma + \tau\text{:\textbf{Type}}$$
$$\Sigma \quad \vdash \quad \mathsf{L}[\sigma]\text{:\textbf{Type}}$$

I will say more about what these types mean shortly. Also, certain parts of HPSG that are not considered here may require additional type constructors (such as a power-type constructor), but in the context of this paper, products, co-products and lists suffice. If $\Sigma \vdash \sigma$:**Type** is derivable, then I refer to σ as a Σ-type.

Features, which are intended to denote maps between the denotations of types, are build from a basic vocabulary of feature symbols together with other operators and punctuation marks. In a type theory of this kind, the technical details regarding the well-formedness of judgements is fairly complicated. But in spirit it is rather straight-forward. First, an assertion of the form $\mathbf{f}{:}\sigma \to \tau$ may be included in Σ provided that $\mathbf{f}$ is a basic feature symbol and σ and τ are both Σ-types. So $\Sigma \vdash \mathbf{f}{:}\sigma \to \tau$ is derivable whenever $\mathbf{f}{:}\sigma \to \tau$ appears in Σ. The assertions of the form $f{:}\sigma \to \tau$ for which $\Sigma \vdash f{:}\sigma \to \tau$ is derivable are closed under operations having to do with (a) behavior of maps in general and (2) the interpretation of products, co-products and lists. In general, if $\Sigma \vdash f{:}\sigma \to \tau$, then I refer to f as a Σ-feature.

For each type σ, $\Sigma \vdash \mathsf{id}_\sigma{:}\sigma \to \sigma$ is derivable. The intended semantics of id_σ is the identity map on σ. If $\Sigma \vdash f{:}\rho \to \sigma$ and $\Sigma \vdash g{:}\sigma \to \tau$ are derivable, then so is $\Sigma \vdash f|g{:}\rho \to \tau$. The intended semantics is the composition of f and g. I take it that the vertical bar is associative. The notation $f|g$ is intended to suggest the concatenation of paths as in feature logic. I could as well have followed the convention of type theory that signifies the composition by $g \circ f$. But the conventions of feature logic and type theory simply clash here.

The type 1 is distinguished as a terminal type. That is, given any other Σ-type σ, there should be exactly one feature from σ to 1. This one feature is denoted by $\Diamond_\sigma : \sigma \to 1$. So $\Sigma \vdash \Diamond_\sigma : \sigma \to 1$ is derivable. Similarly, 0 is distingushed as an initial type. The unique feature from 0 to σ is denoted by $\Box_\sigma : 0 \to \sigma$. For both $\Diamond_\sigma$ and $\Box_\sigma$ the subscript can be omitted when it is understood from context.

The following are derivable for any Σ-types σ and τ

$$\Sigma \quad \vdash \quad \pi_{\sigma,\tau} : \sigma \times \tau \to \sigma$$
$$\Sigma \quad \vdash \quad \pi'_{\sigma,\tau} : \sigma \times \tau \to \tau$$

Again, subscripts can be omitted when context permits. Also, if $\Sigma \vdash f : \rho \to \sigma$ and $\Sigma \vdash g : \rho \to \tau$ are derivable, then so is $\Sigma \vdash \langle f, g \rangle : \rho \to \sigma \times \tau$.

Dually, for any Σ-types σ and τ the following are derivable

$$\Sigma \quad \vdash \quad \iota_{\sigma,\tau} : \sigma \to \sigma + \tau$$
$$\Sigma \quad \vdash \quad \iota'_{\sigma,\tau} : \tau \to \sigma + \tau$$

(subscripts omitted as allowed). If $\Sigma \vdash f : \sigma \to \rho$ and $\Sigma \vdash g : \tau \to \rho$ are derivable, then so is $\Sigma \vdash f, g : (\sigma + \tau) \to \rho$.

Given a Σ-type σ, we also suppose that the Σ-type $\mathsf{L}[\sigma]$ exists and, intuitively at least, is the type of lists with elements drawn from σ. As with products and co-products, lists can be characterized in terms of the existence of certain unique maps. In particular, we suppose that that $\Sigma \vdash \mathsf{nil}_\sigma : 1 \to \mathsf{L}[\sigma]$ and $\Sigma \vdash \mathsf{cons}_\sigma : \sigma \times \mathsf{L}[\sigma] \to \mathsf{L}[\sigma]$ are derivable. What characterizes a list type is that one can define functions (in this context, features) by primitive recursion. In order to keep our meta-theory simple, I formulate primitive recursion with parameters directly. In a richer type theory (in particular with exponents), a primitive recursion scheme with parameters is derivable from a primitive recursion scheme without parameters.

The idea behind a primitive recursion scheme is simply that we can define a feature from $\mathsf{L}[\sigma] \times \rho$ to τ by giving a basic case as a feature $b : \rho \to \tau$ and a recursive case as a feature $r : (\sigma \times \tau) \times \rho \to \tau$. So the theory also requires that if $\Sigma \vdash b : \rho \to \tau$ and $\Sigma \vdash r : (\sigma \times \tau) \times \rho \to \tau$ are derivable, then so is $\Sigma \vdash \mathsf{fold}[b, r] : \mathsf{L}[\sigma] \times \rho \to \tau$.

Equality assertions (those of the form $(f = g) : \sigma \to \tau$) may appear in Σ whenever from $f : \sigma \to \tau$ and $g : \sigma \to \tau$ are Σ-features. Clearly, we would expect that $\Sigma \vdash (f = g) : \sigma \to \tau$ whenever $(f = g) : \sigma \to \tau$ appears in Σ.

Equality assertions codify the provable equalities of features. So derivability is closed under the evident rules that ensure that $=$ behaves as a congruence relation with respect to substitution of equals, and that the features id_σ act as identities, e.g., $\Sigma \vdash (f = f|\mathsf{id}_\tau)\colon \sigma \to \tau$ is derivable for any Σ-feature $f\colon \sigma \to \tau$.

Equality assertions also serve the important function of constraining the possible interpretations of features such as nil and $\langle f, g\rangle$.

If $f\colon \rho \to \sigma$ and $g\colon \rho \to \tau$ are Σ-features, then the following are derivable

$$\Sigma \quad \vdash \quad (f = \langle f, g\rangle \,|\pi)\colon \rho \to \sigma$$
$$\Sigma \quad \vdash \quad (g = \langle f, g\rangle \,|\pi')\colon \rho \to \tau$$

Furthermore, if $\Sigma \vdash m\colon \rho \to \sigma \times \tau$ is derivable, then so is

$$\Sigma \vdash (m = \langle m|\pi, m|\pi'\rangle\colon \rho \to \sigma \times \tau.$$

These rules ensure that (up to derivable equality), $\sigma \times \tau$ is a product with projections π and π'. Similar rules ensure that $\sigma + \tau$ is a co-product and that 1 is a terminal type and 0 is an initial type.

All of the foregoing is fairly routine development of a type theory. But it remains to ensure that $\mathsf{L}[\sigma]$ is constrained so as to be interpretable as a type of lists. In particular, the features nil, cons and fold must be related systematically. The idea that $\mathsf{fold}[b, r]$ should denote a feature defined by recursion can be formulated as follows. If $\Sigma \vdash b\colon \rho \to \tau$ and $\Sigma \vdash r\colon (\sigma \times \tau) \times \rho \to \tau$ are derivable, then so are

$$\Sigma \quad \vdash \quad (\langle \pi|\mathsf{nil}, \pi'\rangle \,|\mathsf{fold}[b, r] = \pi'|b)\colon 1 \times \rho \to \tau$$
$$\Sigma \quad \vdash \quad (\langle \pi|\mathsf{cons}, \pi'\rangle \,|\mathsf{fold}[b, r]$$
$$= \langle\langle \pi|\pi, \langle \pi|\pi', \pi'\rangle \,|\mathsf{fold}[b, r]\rangle, \pi'\rangle \,|r)\colon (\sigma \times \mathsf{L}[\sigma]) \times \rho \to \tau$$

This rather complicated looking specification means, informally, that given an empty list and an element p of ρ, $\mathsf{fold}[b, r]$ yields $b(p)$ and given a non-empty list $(e_0, e_1, \ldots)$ and element of p of ρ, $\mathsf{fold}[b, r]$ yields $r(e_0, \mathsf{fold}[b, r](e_1, \ldots, p), p)$.

We also must insist that $\mathsf{fold}[b, r]$ be the unique feature that meets the above conditions. So, letting f denote the feature $\langle \pi|\mathsf{cons}_\sigma, \pi'\rangle$, if the following are derivable

$$\Sigma \quad \vdash \quad m\colon \mathsf{L}[\sigma] \times \rho \to \tau$$
$$\Sigma \quad \vdash \quad (\langle \pi|\mathsf{nil}_\sigma, \pi'\rangle \,|m = \pi'|b)\colon 1 \times \rho \to \tau$$
$$\Sigma \quad \vdash \quad (f|m = \langle\langle \pi|\pi, \langle \pi|\pi', \pi'\rangle \,|m\rangle, \pi'\rangle \,|r)\colon (\sigma \times \mathsf{L}[\sigma]) \times \rho \to \tau$$

then so is

$$\Sigma \vdash (m = \mathsf{fold}[b, r])\colon \mathsf{L}[\sigma] \times \rho \to \tau.$$

3 Parsing and Grammaticality

A grammar is a set of assumptions about language. In our setting, this translates into a set of formal assumptions Σ about what are the sorts and the features and about what features are equal to one another. We can assume that certain types and features are distinguished. Specifically, *sign* is distinguished as is PHON: *sign* $\to$ *phon* where *phon* is intended as a type that characterizes phonetic representations and PHON is intended as the function that extracts a sign's phonetic realization.

Consider what might we mean by "parsing" in this context. First, of course, we must see what constitutes input to a parser. This is clear enough. Any Σ-feature $u\colon 1 \to phon$ is, essentially, an utterance (according to the type *phon*).

A Σ-*parse* of $u\colon 1 \to phon$ is thus any Σ-feature $p\colon \sigma \to sign$ for which

$$\Sigma \vdash (p|\text{PHON} = \Diamond|u)\colon \sigma \to phon$$

is derivable. Graphically, a parser supplies p and q in the following commutative diagram:

$$
\begin{array}{ccc}
\sigma & \xrightarrow{\ \ q\ \ } & 1 \\
{\scriptstyle p}\big\downarrow & & \big\downarrow{\scriptstyle u} \\
sign & \xrightarrow[\text{PHON}]{} & phon
\end{array}
$$

so that the commutativity of the diagram is derivable from Σ. By definition of 1, $\Sigma \vdash (q = \Diamond_\sigma)\colon \sigma \to 1$ is always derivable So we can simply take q to be $\Diamond_\sigma$ and identify a Σ-parse with p. Notice that by taking σ to be 0, the special case of $p = \square_{sign}$ always yields a Σ-parse, corresponding to a parsing failure.

A Σ-*parser*, then, is an algorithm that takes a Σ-feature $u\colon 1 \to phon$ and returns a Σ-feature $p\colon \sigma \to sign$. It is *correct* provided it always makes the above diagram commute.

A Σ-parser is *complete* if it produces a *most general parse* for any input. That is, suppose that Σ-parse $p\colon \sigma \to sign$ of u is such that for any other Σ-parse $p'\colon \sigma' \to sign$ of u, there is a feature $h\colon \sigma' \to \sigma$ (unique up to derviable equality) for which $\Sigma \vdash (p' = h|p)\colon \sigma \to sign$ is derivable. Also, by definition of 1,

$$\Sigma \vdash (\Diamond_{\sigma'} = h|\Diamond_\sigma)\colon \sigma \to' sign$$

is derivable. We can call p a most general parse, because all other parses of u take the form $h|p$. The idea here is that σ denotes the entire collection of possible parses of u. So if p' is a parse, then p' can be expressed in terms of first mapping to σ and then applying p. If the utterance u is ambiguous, then the most general parse will have σ corresponding informally to a set of signs representing the different analyses of u.

The definitions here yield an interesting variation on the notion of parsing. From the type theoretic perspective, there is nothing special about 1 in the definition of Σ-parses, except that Σ-features from 1 correspond to individuals. Suppose instead that $\hat{u}: \tau \to phon$ is any Σ-feature to *phon*. Think of $\hat{u}$ as a parametric utterance, where values in τ determine the specific utterance. Then we can ask for a Σ-parse of $\hat{u}$, which of course ought to be given by Σ-features $\hat{p}: \sigma \to sign$ and $\hat{q}: \sigma \to \tau$ making the diagram

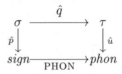

commute.

The notion of a parametric parse provides an account of what a linguist does in a typical argument from data. That is, the familiar lists of grammaticality judgements are intended as representative of a class of utterances, which vary along some parameter. This can be thought of generally as a function $\hat{u}$ from some type to phonetic representations. Then based on grammaticality judgements (and perhaps other data and assumptions), the linguist argues that a parametric parse for $\hat{u}$ must meet various conditions, hence Σ must include assumptions that allow those conditions to be met.

Consider the following simple illustration. Suppose that due to earlier arguments, we have concluded that certain signs can be singled out as playing the role of noun phrases. That is, $\Sigma \vdash$ NP: $np \to sign$ is derivable. Of course, this is not enough to characterize noun phrases, but it suffices for this illustration. Now consider the "parametric utterance" $\hat{w}: np \to phon$ which simply appends the utterance *wok* to the phonetic representation of a noun phrase. In other words, it takes a noun phrase x and produces $\text{PHON}(\text{NP}(x))\frown wok$. Some of the data produced by $\hat{w}$ can be illustrated orthographically by

(i) I walk.

(ii) You walk.

(iii) *He walk.

(iv) We walk.

(v) You walk.

(vi) They walk.

The asterisk on (iii) indicates that in a parametric parse of $\hat{w}$, the noun phrase that precedes *wok* cannot be a sign corresponding to "he." That is, if HE: $he \to np$ is a feature which picks out the noun phrases corresponding to the masculine, second person singular pronoun. Then the only Σ-parse of HE$|\hat{w}$ is

$$
\begin{array}{ccc}
0 & \xrightarrow{\;\Box_{he}\;} & he \\[2pt]
{\scriptstyle\Box_{sign}}\Big\downarrow & & \Big\downarrow{\scriptstyle \text{HE}|\hat{w}} \\[2pt]
sign & \xrightarrow[\text{PHON}]{} & phon
\end{array}
$$

So this tells us something substantive about possible Σ-parses of $\hat{w}$. Namely, if $\hat{q}$ factors through HE, then in fact the parse is a failure. More generally, there is an entire class of noun phrases, all characterized as third person, singular, that cannot precede *wok* in this context. If we already have recognized the variation of person and number in noun phrases, then this parametric parse suggests that *wok* (and by similar parametric parses that vary the verb, all intransitive verbs) control the number and person of their subjects in a particular way in English. This is, of course, the beginning of the notion of agreement.

If we assume that a sign also has MEANING: $sign \to meaning$, a distinguished feature taking a sign to its meaning, then we can also consider generation in the specific and parametric cases as the construction of a Σ-feature to signs from a feature $m\colon \tau \to meaning$ so as to make the diagram

$$
\begin{array}{ccc}
\sigma & \xrightarrow{\;\hat{q}\;} & \tau \\[2pt]
{\scriptstyle\hat{p}}\Big\downarrow & & \Big\downarrow{\scriptstyle \hat{m}} \\[2pt]
sign & \xrightarrow[\text{MEANING}]{} & meaning
\end{array}
$$

commute.

4 Principles as Universals

The idea behind, e.g., the Head Feature Principle is that, in order to make a wide range of parametric parses jibe with the data, signs possess a feature that is systematically shared between a headed phrase and its head daughter. This is easily formulated in assumptions by insisting that

$$\Sigma \;\vdash\; head\text{:}\textbf{Type}$$

$$\Sigma \;\vdash\; hdd\text{-}phr\text{:}\textbf{Type}$$

$$\Sigma \;\vdash\; \text{HEAD: } sign \to head$$

$$\Sigma \;\vdash\; \text{HD-DTR: } hdd\text{-}phrase \to sign$$

$$\Sigma \;\vdash\; \text{HDD-PHR: } hdd\text{-}phr \to sign$$

$$\Sigma \ \vdash \ (\text{HD-DTR}|\text{HEAD} = \text{HDD-PHR}|\text{HEAD}): \textit{hdd-phr} \rightarrow \textit{head}$$

Writing HFP for this set of six judgements, the claim that the Head Feature Principle holds is simply the assertion that in any grammar of a human language, HFP is derivable. Similar sets of assumptions correspond to other HPSG principles such as the Subcategorization Principle (SP). But I return to this later.

Usually, the claim that HFP and SP are "universal" simply means that (whatever their formalization) they hold in every grammar of a human language. But there is another technical meaning to the word "universal" that bears on the role of theoretically motivated types such as *head* and *synsem*. Any characteristic of signs that is systematically identical in a sign and its head daughter is justifiably accounted for within the type *head*. That is, *head* does not merely account for some of the characteristics of signs that are shared by a sign and its daughter, rather *head* is meant to capture exactly those characteristics and nothing else. Similarly, *synsem* is meant to capture exactly those characteristics of signs that can be selected for. The idea that these sorts capture exactly some characteristic of signs can be made precise through the category theoretic notion of a "universal arrow." The HEAD feature illustrates the idea.

We expect the HFP judgements to be derivable. But further, suppose that

$$\Sigma \vdash (\text{HEAD-DTR}|f = \text{HEADED-PHRASE}|f): \textit{headed-phrase} \rightarrow \sigma$$

is derivable for some Σ-feature f. That is in words, f picks out some characteristic of signs, the values of which are drawn from σ, and this characteristic is shared between any headed phrase and its head daughter. On the basis of this equality, we would be inclined to invent a new feature, say $h\colon \textit{head} \rightarrow \sigma$, and require that f be derivably equal to HEAD$|h$.

For a concrete example, let *cat* be a type that represents the standard grammatical categories. Also, let CAT: $\textit{sign} \rightarrow \textit{cat}$ be a Σ-feature that assigns a category to every sign. Through various arguments (essentially arguments supporting $\bar{X}$ theory), a linguist would conclude that

$$\Sigma \vdash (\text{HD-DTR}|\text{CAT} = \text{HDD-PHR}|\text{CAT}): \textit{hdd-phr} \rightarrow \textit{cat}$$

ought to be derivable. That is, the category associated with a headed phrase is (according to the grammar Σ) always the same as the category associated with the phrase's head daughter. In standard HPSG, this justifies *removal* of the feature CAT from being appropriate for *sign* to being appropriate for *head*. But in this type theoretic account, it argues that Σ should be such that there is a Σ-feature hd[CAT]: $\textit{head} \rightarrow \textit{cat}$, unique up to derivable equality, so that

$$\Sigma \vdash (\text{CAT} = \text{HEAD}|\text{hd}[\text{CAT}]): sign \to cat$$

is derivable.

A similar argument can be made for any Σ-feature $f: sign \to \sigma$ that makes HDD-PHR and HD-DTR agree: for any such f, we would be justified in introducing a feature $\text{hd}[f]$ appropriate to *head* so that f can be written as $\text{HEAD}|\text{hd}[f]$ (the notation $\text{hd}[f]$ is simply meant to indicate that this new feature $\text{hd}[f]$ depends only on f). This argues that HEAD is what is known in category theory as a *co-equalizer* of HEAD-DTR and HEADED-PHRASE, or more generically, a *universal feature* making HEAD-DTR and HEADED-PHRASE agree.

Thus, the universal character of the HFP suggests that the type theory be extended so that

$$\Sigma \quad \vdash \quad head:\textbf{Type}$$
$$\Sigma \quad \vdash \quad \text{HEAD}: sign \to head$$
$$\Sigma \quad \vdash \quad (\text{HD-DTR}|\text{HEAD} = \text{HDD-PHR}|\text{HEAD}): hdd\text{-}phr \to \sigma$$

are derivable (so far the type theory can provide this) and so that if

$$\Sigma \vdash (\text{HD-DTR}|f = \text{HDD-PHR}|f): hdd\text{-}phr \to \sigma$$

is derivable, then so are

$$\Sigma \quad \vdash \quad \text{hd}[f]: head \to \sigma$$
$$\Sigma \quad \vdash \quad f = \text{HEAD}|\text{hd}[f]: sign \to \sigma$$

Furthermore, to ensure uniqueness of HEAD we must also insist that if $m: head \to \sigma$ is a Σ-feature, then $\Sigma \vdash (m = \text{hd}[\text{HEAD}|m]): head \to \sigma$ must be derivable. In other words, the Head Feature Principle can be precisely formalized in the way that it is typically used informally— as a requirement that any feature that is established as systematically being shared between a headed phrase and its head daughter must factor through the "official" head feature. Notice that the formalization of the HFP requires that the simple type theory be extended. This may be a useful point to consider. Namely, the informal argumentation that centers on feature geometry (such as placement of features under *head*) appears by necessity to involve stronger meta-theoretical machinery than the simpler job of writing constraints on features.

The Subcategorization Principle requires that the following be derivable:

$$\Sigma \quad \vdash \quad \text{SYNSEM}: sign \to synsem$$
$$\Sigma \quad \vdash \quad \text{SUBCAT}: sign \to \mathsf{L}[synsem]$$

$$\Sigma \vdash (\text{HD-DTR}|\text{SUBCAT}$$

$$= \langle \begin{array}{l} \text{HDD-PHR}|\text{SUBCAT}, \\ \text{COMP-DTRS}|\text{L}[\text{SYNSEM}] \end{array} \quad \rangle |\text{concat}):sign \to \text{L}[synsem]$$

where COMP-DTRS: $hdd\text{-}phr \to \text{L}[sign]$ picks out a headed phrase's complement daughters, concat is the concatenator for lists of $synsem$ elements (defined as $\text{fold}[\text{id}, \pi|\text{cons}]$), and $\text{L}[f]\colon \text{L}[\sigma] \to \text{L}[\tau]$ is the "map" feature of standard list processing (also defined via fold).

Like the Head Feature Principle, the Subcategorization Principle can be regarded as a definition. Specifically, $synsem$ denotes the characteristics of signs that can be selected for in subcategorization. Subcategorization amounts to finding a list of values for a head daughter so that that list of values consists of the subcategorization list of the headed phrase itself and the concatenation of values for all complement daughters. So the general picture of subcategorization phenomena is summed up in the following diagram:

$$
\begin{array}{ccc}
 & \langle \text{HDD-PHR}|s, \text{COMP-DTRS}|\text{L}[c] \rangle & \\
hdd\text{-}phr \xrightarrow{\hspace{3cm}} & \text{L}[\sigma] \times \text{L}[\sigma] \\
\text{HD-DTR} \Big\downarrow & & \Big\downarrow \text{concat} \\
sign \xrightarrow{\hspace{2cm} s \hspace{2cm}} & \text{L}[\sigma]
\end{array}
$$

where $s\colon sign \to \text{L}[\sigma]$ and $c\colon sign \to \sigma$ are any Σ-features that make the diagram commute (according to Σ). For example, a first approximation to subcategorization assigns a list of categories to each sign. Let SUB-CAT: $sign \to \text{L}[cat]$ denote the feature that assigns subcategorization with respect to category alone to each sign. So to the sign corresponding to an intransitive verb, SUB-CAT might simply assign the single element list consisting of n (the sign subcategorizes for a noun phrase). Once again, based on parametric parses, we would claim that

$$
\begin{array}{ccc}
 & \langle \text{HDD-PHR}|\text{SUB-CAT}, \text{COMP-DTRS}|\text{L}[\text{CAT}] \rangle & \\
hdd\text{-}phr \xrightarrow{\hspace{3cm}} & \text{L}[cat] \times \text{L}[cat] \\
\text{HD-DTR} \Big\downarrow & & \Big\downarrow \text{concat} \\
sign \xrightarrow{\hspace{2cm} \text{SUB-CAT} \hspace{2cm}} & \text{L}[cat]
\end{array}
$$

should be derivable. In words, heads subcategorize for category.

If SYNSEM and SUBCAT characterize all facts about subcategorization, then the above observation leads us to require a Σ-feature

$$\text{ss}[\text{CAT}, \text{SUB-CAT}]\colon synsem \to cat$$

so that the following are derivable:

$$\Sigma \vdash (\text{CAT} = \text{SYNSEM}|\text{ss}[\text{CAT}, \text{SUB-CAT}])\colon sign \to cat$$

$$\Sigma \vdash (\text{SUB-CAT} = \text{SUBCAT}|\text{L}[\text{ss}[\text{CAT}, \text{SUB-CAT}]]): sign \to \text{L}[cat]$$

and so that this feature is unique up to derivable equality.

This suggests that, in addition to the simple Subcategorization Principle, we should require that $\langle \text{SUBCAT}, \text{SYNSEM} \rangle$ be the universal feature meeting the Subcategorization Principle. Again, the apparatus needed for this is available by extending the type theory. That is, letting f denote the feature $\langle \text{HDD-PHR}|\text{SUB-CAT}, \text{COMP-DTRS}|\text{L}[c] \rangle$, if

$$\Sigma \vdash (f|\text{concat} = \text{HD-DTR}|s): hdd\text{-}phr \to \text{L}[\sigma]$$

is derivable, then so are all of

$$\Sigma \quad \vdash \quad \text{ss}[c, s]: synsem \to \sigma$$
$$\Sigma \quad \vdash \quad (c = \text{SYNSEM}|\text{ss}[c, s]): sign \to \sigma$$
$$\Sigma \quad \vdash \quad (s = \text{SUBCAT}|\text{L}[\text{ss}[c, s]]): sign \to \text{L}[\sigma]$$

And if $m: synsem \to \sigma$ is a Σ-feature so that

$$\Sigma \quad \vdash \quad (c = \text{SYNSEM}|m): sign \to \sigma$$

$$Sigma \quad \vdash \quad (s = \text{SUBCAT}|\text{L}[m]): sign \to \text{L}[\sigma]$$

then $\Sigma \vdash (m = \text{ss}[c, s]): synsem \to \sigma$ is derivable.

As with the Head Feature Principle, the type theory extended to account for subcategorization formalizes precisely the role that features SYNSEM and SUBCAT and sort *synsem* play in determining feature geometry.

5 The Lexicon

The details of how a lexicon is organized is one of the least elegant parts of HPSG. The role of lexical rules is not clear. The status of a "lexical entry" is difficult to characterize because of a tension between the desire to think of feature structures (the representations of signs) as non-partial objects and the need to capture regularities in the lexicon as partial constraints. It seems that the things in a lexicon must not be signs, for signs are represented by totally defined objects, yet the data that is captured in a lexicon is partial.

An idea similar to that of parametric parse, as suggested in Section 3, can be used to gain a purchase on the organization of a lexicon. Recall that a specific parse involved input of the form $u: 1 \to phon$, whereas a parametric parse involved input of the form $\hat{u}: \sigma \to phon$. In a similar vein, a *specific sign* is a Σ-feature $s: 1 \to sign$ whereas a *parametric sign* is a Σ-feature $\hat{s}: \sigma \to sign$. Think of $\hat{s}$ as producing a specific sign from parameters drawn from σ.

Now, the lexicon can be organized as a collection of parametric signs. For example, DOG: $dog \to sign$ might be a lexical entry for "dog" where dog codifies the variations in meanings and usage involved in the word "dog." Thus, the type dog would represent just exactly what all "dog" signs have in common. For example, we might expect dog to be isomorphic to $number \times \sigma$ for some σ in order to capture the fact that the common noun "dog" can vary along number: "dog" and "dogs" are the same word (part of the same parametric sign).

So what we typically regard as individual words (lexical entries) constitute parametric signs (Σ-features that take values in $sign$). The facts that hold about a word (its subcategorization, its meaning, etc.) are encoded in assumptions about how the parametric sign figures in various commutative diagrams.

With this basic picture of the lexicon as a collection of parametric signs (or more accurately, as a set of assumptions in Σ about parametric signs), the organization of the lexicon becomes quite interesting. Parametric signs are not restricted to things that we usually regard as words. For example, CN: $cn \to sign$ might be a parametric sign representing common nouns. Assumptions about CN constitute our knowledge of what characteristics are shared by all common nouns. In fact, if common nouns have a precise characterization in terms of commutative diagrams, then we could choose to define CN as a universal feature, by methods similar to the definition of HEAD, for those commutative diagrams. Thus, if parametric sign DOG: $dog \to sign$ meets specific commutativity conditions then it is a common noun, i.e., DOG factors uniquely through CN.

Lexical rules can also be accounted for. Consider the passivization rule. In standard HPSG it acts on lexical entries as a sort of closure operator on the lexicon. That is, if an entry meets certain conditions (essentially it must represent an active verb), then the passivization rule adds another entry to the lexicon representing the active verbs passive version.

From the type theoretic perspective advocated here, the passivization rule is simply another Σ-feature PASS: $active \to passive$, where ACT: $active \to sign$ and PSV: $passive \to sign$ are the parametric signs corresponding to active and passive verbs. The details of exactly how PASS relates active to passive is, of course, codified in Σ.

6 The Type Theory

In this section, I set out a formal definition of the type theory. The judgements of the theory take the form $\Sigma \vdash \phi$ where Σ is a (finite) set of assertions, subject to certain well-formedness conditions, and ϕ is an assertion. Well-formedness conditions for the antecedent Σ are as follows.

1. $\emptyset$ is a well-formed antecedent;

2. if Σ is well-formed and s does not appear in Σ, then $s : \mathbf{Type}, \Sigma$ is a well-formed antecedent;

3. if Σ is a well-formed antecedent, and both $\Sigma \vdash \tau : \mathbf{Type}$ and $\Sigma \vdash \tau : \mathbf{Type}$ are derivable, and f does not appear in Σ, then $f : \sigma \to \tau, \Sigma$ is a well-formed antecedent; and

4. if Σ is a well-formed antecedent, and both $\Sigma \vdash f : \sigma \to \tau$ and $\Sigma \vdash g : \sigma \to \tau$ are derivable, then $f = g : \sigma \to \tau, \Sigma$ is a well-formed antecedent.

Derivations allow for identity axioms, weakening of antecedents, and cuts (all subject to the well-formedness of antecedents. That is,

1. If ϕ, Σ is a well-formed antecedent, then $\phi, \Sigma \vdash \phi$ is derivable; and

2. if Σ and ψ, Σ are both well-formed antecedents, and $\Sigma \vdash \phi$ is derivable, then so is $\psi, \Sigma \vdash \phi$; and

3. if $\Sigma \vdash \phi$ and $\phi, \Sigma' \vdash \psi$ are both derivable, and Σ, Σ' is a well-formed antecedent, then $\Sigma, \Sigma' \vdash \psi$ is derivable.

Judgements of the form $\Sigma \vdash \sigma : \mathbf{Type}$ are derivable subject to the following conditions.

$\Sigma \vdash \ldots$ is derivable	Subject to $\Sigma \vdash \ldots$
$1 : \mathbf{Type}$	
$(\sigma \times \tau) : \mathbf{Type}$	$\sigma : \mathbf{Type}$ and $\tau : \mathbf{Type}$
$(\sigma + \tau) : \mathbf{Type}$	$\sigma : \mathbf{Type}$ and $\tau : \mathbf{Type}$
$0 : \mathbf{Type}$	
$\mathsf{L}[\sigma] : \mathbf{Type}$	$\sigma : \mathbf{Type}$

These judgements can easily be proved to depend only on the type assertions appearing in Σ, in the sense that if $\Sigma \vdash \sigma : \mathbf{Type}$ is derivable, then Σ can be written as Σ', Σ'' so that (i) Σ'' contains only type assertions, (ii) $\Sigma'' \vdash \sigma : \mathbf{Type}$ is derivable without the use of weakening or cut, and (iii) $\Sigma', \Sigma'' \vdash \sigma : \mathbf{Type}$ is derivable from $\Sigma'' \vdash \sigma : \mathbf{Type}$ by a series of weakenings.

Judgements of the form $\Sigma \vdash f : \sigma \to \tau$ are derivable subject to the following conditions.

$\Sigma \vdash \ldots$ is derivable	Subject to $\Sigma \vdash \ldots$
$f\|g: \rho \to \tau$	$f: \rho \to \sigma$ and
	$g: \sigma \to \tau$
$\mathsf{id}_\sigma: \sigma \to \sigma$	$\sigma\!:\!\mathbf{Type}$
$\pi_{\sigma,\tau}: \sigma \times \tau \to \sigma$	$\sigma\!:\!\mathbf{Type}$ and $\tau\!:\!\mathbf{Type}$
$\pi'_{\sigma,\tau}: \sigma \times \tau \to \tau$	$\sigma\!:\!\mathbf{Type}$ and $\tau\!:\!\mathbf{Type}$
$\langle f, g \rangle : \rho \to \sigma \times \tau$	$f: \rho \to \sigma$ and $g: \rho \to \tau$
$\diamondsuit_\sigma: \sigma \to 1$	$\sigma\!:\!\mathbf{Type}$
$\iota_{\sigma,\tau}: \sigma \to \sigma + \tau$	$\sigma\!:\!\mathbf{Type}$ and $\tau\!:\!\mathbf{Type}$
$\iota'_{\sigma,\tau}: \tau \to \sigma \times \tau$	$\sigma\!:\!\mathbf{Type}$ and $\tau\!:\!\mathbf{Type}$
$[f, g]: \sigma \times \tau \to \rho$	$f: \sigma \to \rho$ and $g: \tau \to \rho$
$\square_\sigma: 0 \to \sigma$	$\sigma\!:\!\mathbf{Type}$
$\mathsf{nil}_\sigma: 1 \to \mathsf{L}[\sigma]$	$\sigma\!:\!\mathbf{Type}$
$\mathsf{cons}_\sigma: \sigma \times \mathsf{L}[\sigma] \to \mathsf{L}[\sigma]$	$\sigma\!:\!\mathbf{Type}$
$\mathsf{fold}[n, c]: \mathsf{L}[\sigma] \times \rho \to \tau$	$n: \rho \to \tau$ and $c: (\sigma \times \tau) \times \rho \to \tau$

As with type assertions, judgements with feature assertions as conclusions can be shown to depend only on type assertions and feature assertions in Σ. To wit, if $\Sigma \vdash f: \sigma \to \tau$, then Σ can be written as Σ', Σ'' so that (i) Σ'' is a well-formed antecedent consisting only of type and feature assertions, (ii) $\Sigma'' \vdash f: \sigma \to \tau$ is derivable without the use of weakening or cut, and (iii) $\Sigma', \Sigma'' \vdash f: \sigma \to \tau$ is derivable from $\Sigma'' \vdash f: \sigma \to \tau$ by a series of weakenings.

Also note that if $x: \sigma \to \tau, \Sigma \vdash F(x): \rho \to \upsilon$ and $\Sigma \vdash f: \sigma \to \tau$ are both derivable, then $\Sigma \vdash F(f): \rho \to \upsilon$ is also derivable, where $F(f)$ is obtained by replacing all occurences of x in $F(x)$ by f.

Finally, judgements of the form $\Sigma \vdash f = g: \sigma \to \tau$ are subject to the following conditions. The first three conditions, we can consider separately, as they have to do with equality as a congruence relation.

$\Sigma \vdash \ldots$ is derivable	Subject to $\Sigma \vdash \ldots$
$f = f: \sigma \to \tau$	$f: \sigma \to \tau$
$f = h: \sigma \to \tau$	$f = g: \sigma \to \tau$ and $g = h: \sigma \to \tau$
$f = g: \sigma \to \tau$	$g = h: \sigma \to \tau$
$F(f) = F(g): \rho \to \upsilon$	$f = g: \sigma \to \tau$

where $x: \sigma \to \tau, \Sigma \vdash F(x): \rho \to \upsilon$ is derivable. Finally, judgements of the form $\Sigma \vdash f = g: \sigma \to \tau$ are subject to conditions that formalize the intended meanings of constructed features.

$\Sigma \vdash \ldots$ is derivable	Subject to $\Sigma \vdash \ldots$
$f = \mathsf{id}_\sigma \| f : \sigma \to \tau$	$f : \sigma \to \tau$
$f = f \| \mathsf{id}_\tau : \sigma \to \tau$	$f : \sigma \to \tau$
$f = \langle f, g \rangle \| \pi : \rho \to \sigma$	$f : \rho \to \sigma$ and $g : \rho \to \tau$
$g = \langle f, g \rangle \| \pi' : \rho \to \tau$	$f : \rho \to \sigma$ and $g : \rho \to \tau$
$m = \langle m \| \pi, m \| \pi' \rangle : \rho \to \sigma \times \tau$	$m : \rho \to \sigma \times \tau$
$\diamondsuit_\sigma = m : \sigma \to 1$	$m : \sigma \to 1$
$f = \iota \| [f, g] : \sigma \to \rho$	$f : \sigma \to \rho$ and $g : \tau \to \rho$
$g = \iota' \| [f, g] : \tau \to \rho$	$f : \sigma \to \rho$ and $g : \tau \to \rho$
$m = [\iota \| m, \iota' \| m] : \sigma + \tau \to \rho$	$m : \sigma + \tau \to \rho$
$\square_\sigma = m : 0 \to \sigma$	$\Sigma \vdash m : 0 \to \sigma$
$\pi \| n = N \| \mathsf{fold}[n, c] : 1 \times \rho \to \tau$	$n : \rho \to \tau$ and $c : (\sigma \times \tau) \times \rho \to$
$R(\mathsf{fold}[n, c]) \| c = C \| \mathsf{fold}[n, c]$ $: (\sigma \times \mathsf{L}[\sigma]) \times \rho \to \tau$	$n : \rho \to \tau$ and $c : (\sigma \times \tau) \times \rho \to \tau$
$m = \mathsf{fold}[N \| m, c] : \mathsf{L}[\sigma] \times \rho \to \tau$	$R(m) \| c = C \| m$ $: (\sigma \times \mathsf{L}[\sigma]) \times \rho \to \tau$

where N abbreviates $\langle \pi \| \mathsf{nil}, \pi' \rangle$, C abbreviates $\langle \pi \| \mathsf{cons}, \pi' \rangle$, and the expression $R(h)$ abbreviates $\langle \langle \pi \| \pi, \langle \pi \| \pi', \pi' \rangle \| h \rangle, \pi' \rangle$ for any feature h from $\mathsf{L}[\sigma]$ to τ. The type theory enjoys a strong normalization property is the sense that we can take the equality assertions shown in the last table as determining a normal form for features. That is, say that a derivable judgement $\Sigma \vdash g : \sigma \to \tau$, is *in normal form* if g does not contain any subexpressions that are of the forms found on the right hand sides of any of the equality assertions in the last table. If $\Sigma \vdash f : \sigma \to \tau$ is derivable, then there is a derivable judgement $\Sigma \vdash f = g : \sigma \to \tau$ so that $\Sigma \vdash g : \sigma \to \tau$ is in normal form. Furthermore, if Σ contains no equality assertions, then g is unique. The result is easily obtained by first observing that the cut rule and the rules of derivation to do with congruence of the equals sign can be eliminated up to assertions appearing in Σ (cuts and congruence rules involving members of Σ can not necessarily be eliminated). If Σ does not contain any equality assertions, then all uses of the cut rule and the congruence rules can be eliminated, thus reducing the problem to an induction on the "degree" of a feature.

7 Conclusion

I have defined a type theory that is rich enough to allow the formalization of HPSG as a collection of assumptions about types. From this, I have briefly sketched (a) how HPSG principles can be formulated in the type theory, (b) how parsing as an algorithm to produce (sets of) signs from utterances can be formulated and generalized to account for a standard form of linguistic argumentation, (c) how certain HPSG principles and definitions are special cases of a common category theoretic notion of universality, (d) how universality captures the informal reasoning that occurs in standard HPSG regarding feature geometry, and (e) how the type theoretic approach to the HPSG lexicon solves problems with the status of lexical entries and lexical rules within a grammar.

Although I have concentrated my arguments on HPSG, they are just as applicable to other linguistic theories, particularly Lexical Functional Grammar. Even more interesting is the fact that the type theoretic approach I have taken here meshes well with, e.g., Montagovian semantics, and thus may ultimately find useful connections to Categorial Grammar.

Some practical questions arise from the standard concerns of HPSG (and Lexical Functional Grammar) regarding procedural interpretation of a grammar: Can a set of assumptions be treated as a specification for a *realistic* parser. I've indicated how such a set can be treated as a specification for a rather abstract parser, but of course, that is a long way from an implementation. The work involved in producing an actual parser will essentially be the work needed for a theorem prover for the type theory. The formalism is "fully-typed" in the sense that the types of features are carried with them. But in practical use, one does not want to have to explicitly state types with every mention of an expression. Thus, type inference is an important practical matter that must be investigated.

In this paper, I have argued that a common kind of argumentation that occurs in HPSG can be given a formal basis. This argumentation has to do with feature geometry and typically invokes some special (informal) understanding of the significance of certain sorts and features. By formulating HPSG in terms of type theory — essentially generalizing on feature logic seen as a simple type theory — this otherwise informal understanding of significance can be made completely formal. Furthermore, the concepts (products, co-products and lists) used in the basic type theory are all quite well understood in the context of constructive mathematics. The advantage to this is that many of the familiar concerns of linguistics, such as parsing, lexical rules, lexical entries, universal principles, decisions regarding "architecture" of signs, are seen to be closely related and in many instances overlapping. The result is a conceptually simple formalism that is strong enough to formalize large parts of HPSG, and that provides a bridge to the broader field of constructive mathematics.

References

Beeson, Michael. 1985. *Foundations of Constructive Mathematics.* New York:Springer-Verlag.

van Benthem, Johan. 1983. Determiners and Logic. In *Linguistics and Philosophy*, Volume 6, pages 664–478.

Calcagno, Michael. 1993. Toward a linearization-based approach to word order variation in Japanese. In Andreas Kathol and Carl Pollard, editors, *Papers in Syntax*, number 42 in OSU Working Papers in Linguistics, pages 26–45. Department of Linguistics, Ohio State University.

Carpenter, Bob. 1992. *The Logic of Typed Feature Structures with Applications to Unification-based Grammars, Logic Programming and Constraint Resolution.* Cambridge Tracts in Theoretical Computer Science, vol 23. Cambridge: Cambridge University Press.

Dalrymple, Mary, John Lamping, Fernando C. N. Pereira and Vijay Saraswat. 1996. A Deductive Account of Quantification in LFG. In M. Kanazawa, C. Piñòn, H. de Swart, eds. *Quantifiers, Deduction and Context*, 33–58. Palo Alto: CSLI Publications.

Gazdar, Gerald, Ewan Klein, Geoff Pullum and Ivan Sag. 1985. *Generalized Phrase Structure Grammar.* Oxford: Basil Blackwell.

Keenan, Edward, and Lawrence Faltz. 1985. *Boolean Semantics for Natural Language.* Synthese Language Library, vol. 23, Dordrecht: Reidel.

King, Paul. 1989. *A Logical Formalism for Head-Driven Phrase Structure Grammar.* Doctoral dissertation, University of Manchester.

Lambek, Joachim. 1961. On the Calculus of Syntactic Types. In R. Jakobson, ed., *Structure of Language and its Mathematical Aspects*, 166–178. Providence: American Mathematical Society.

Moshier, M. Andrew. 1997. Featureless HPSG. In P. Blackburn and M. de Rijke, eds., *Specifying Syntactic Structures.* Palo Alto: CSLI Publications.

Moshier, M. Andrew. 1997. Is HPSG featureless or unprincipled? *Linguistics and Philosophy*, to appear.

Morrill, Glynn. 1994. *Type Logical Grammar* Dordrecht: Kluwer.

Netter, Klaus. 1994. Towards a theory of functional heads. In John Nerbonne, Klaus Netter, and Carl Pollard, editors, *German in Head-Driven Phrase Structure Grammar*, Lecture Notes number 46, 297–340. Palo Alto: CSLI Publications.

Oliva, Karel. 1992. The proper treatment of word order in HPSG. In *Proceedings of Coling 92*, 184–190. Nantes.

Pollard, Carl and Ivan A. Sag. 1994. *Head-Driven Phrase Structure Grammar.* Chicago: University of Chicago Press.

7

Machine Learning of Physics Word Problems: A Preliminary Report

PATRICK SUPPES, MICHAEL BÖTTNER AND LIN LIANG

1 Introduction

In this article we continue the research on machine learning of natural language begun in Suppes et al. 1992, which is the first publication, although the research started in 1989. Until recently we have concentrated on a natural robotic language for elementary assembly actions (Suppes et al. 1995, Suppes et al. 1995). In the present article we turn to machine learning of physics word problems. The same basic axioms of learning are used for these rather different uses of language. In spite of the considerable interest in physics word problems by cognitive scientists (e.g., Larkin 1983), many of the persuasion that human beings are, above all, formal symbol processors, no sustained effort, as far as we know, has previously been made to study in detail what conceptual apparatus is needed to read such problems and produce as output the desired equations. Bobrow's system STUDENT (1964) dealt with high school algebra word problems, but had no machine learning component. The report of our first efforts to construct such a machine-learning program is given here. As will be evident, the results are certainly preliminary, but they do reflect our more extensive past experience with the machine learning of robotic language.

We emphasize that our machine-learning program, which has been applied to ten natural languages (see the references), assumes no prior knowledge of the target language. The only given knowledge is an alphabet and the fact that a word is an unbroken string of letters of the alphabet. It does have an internal language, essentially a language for physical equations, that is far removed from any given natural language,

Computing Natural Language.
Atocha Aliseda, Rob van Glabbeek, and Dag Westerståhl, editors.
Copyright © 1998, Stanford University.

and in particular from English. Details of this internal language are given in Section 2. Key notions of our learning theory are working memory, long-term mempry, association, generalization, denotational value, and memory trace. These central concepts of our theory are explained in detail in Section 3, together with examples sketching their application to physics word problems. Here we remark on their intuitive origin.

The concept of generalization is widely used in psychological theories of learning. The principle of association goes back at least to Aristotle, and certainly was used extensively by eighteenth-century philosophers like Hume long before psychology had become an experimental science. The fundamental role of association as a basis for conditioning is thoroughly recognized in modern neuroscience and is essential to the experimental study of the neuronal activity of a variety of animals. For similar reasons its role is just as central to the learning theory of neural networks, now rapidly developing in many different directions. Our distinction about kinds of memory is standard in psychological studies of human memory, but the details of our machine-learning process are not necessarily faithful to human learning of language, and we make no claim that they are. On the other hand, our basic processes of association, generalization, specification and rule generation almost certainly have analogues in human learning, some better understood than others at the present time. In the general axioms formulated in this section we assume rather little about the specific language of the internal representation, although the examples that illustrate the axioms use the internal language described in section 2.

Another notion that is characteristic of our approach to learning is the concept of a denotational value. The denotational value of a word is the probability of whether that word has a denotation relative to the specific semantics of the problem domain. Not all words have a denotation relative to the given semantics. Which words have a denotation is largely determined by the internal language. In the robotic case our internal language has objects, properties, spatial relations, and actions. Therefore words not denoting anything that belongs to one of these categories are non-denoting. It is one of the purposes of learning to distinguish denoting words from nondenoting words. Before learning occurs a denotational value of 1 is assigned to every word. This value then gets reduced for non-denoting words during learning.

Section 4 summarizes our preliminary results and discusses some problems expected to arise. A formal statement of our learning axioms is given in the appendix.

2   Internal Language

As in the case of our work on robotic language, we concentrate on language learning and not on concept formation. This means that we endow the program with an internal language having a well-defined grammar and semantics. This internal language is not learned. It is used to interpret and learn the natural language,—in the present case English—, used to formulate physics word problems.

The internal language formulated here is for simple one-dimensional kinematic problems, but can easily be extended to cover other physics problems. The important point is that it is essentially an equational language, in which the reasoning is about equations, especially about the equations that express the data of a problem such as initial and final conditions, which may be formulated for a variety of physical quantities.

In the elementary problems which we have studied, the basic background assumptions are these. (i) Only kinematics of bodies is analyzed; no dynamics. (ii) Physical bodies are treated as point particles. (iii) Acceleration is always at a constant or uniform rate. (iv) The problems are all of one spatial dimension. (v) No derivatives of positions or velocity are introduced. Consequently the only relevant data or answers to questions are in terms of the following physical quantities: initial time t_0, initial position x_0, initial velocity $v(t_0)$; final time t_1, final position x_1, final velocity $v(t_1)$; elapsed distance Δx, elapsed time Δt; change in velocity Δv; acceleration a. So we can write in the internal language physical equations such as

$$v(t) = 10 \ m/s, \qquad x_o = 5.1 \ m,$$
$$t_1 = 60.2 \ s, \qquad \Delta t = 5 \ s.$$

where m is the symbol for *meters*, s for seconds, v for velocity, and t for time.

In contradistinction to the robotic language we have no category of objects. At the level of physics considered here all bodies are considered as point particles, and so we do not differentiate between properties of cars, trucks, tricycles and balls, because mass or weight is not a kinematical property. This is an important kind of abstraction used in physics, one which students must learn to do word problems efficiently.

Here is a very simple problem to illustrate our method of analysis. We directly give the representation in the internal language used to make semantic computations.

$$A \quad car \quad accelerates \quad from \qquad 3.1 \ m/s$$
$$(t_0 = t \quad \& \quad v(t) = 3.1 \ m/s)$$

$$to \qquad 6.9 \; m/s \qquad in \qquad 5.0 \; s.$$
$$(t_1 = t \quad \& \quad v(t) = 6.9 \; m/s) \quad (\Delta t = q \quad \& \quad q = 5.0 \; s)$$

$$What \quad is \quad its \quad acceleration?$$
$$a(t) =?$$

The constant t_0 in the equation $t_0 = t$ is one of the semantic interpretations of *from*, special for physics word problems. The term $3.1 \; m/s$ in the equation $v(t) = 3.1 \; m/s$ is the same in the internal representation. We use the units to determine the physical quantity v, but the time argument is left variable, to be determined by using the interpretation of *from* or *to*. Thus, the phrase *from* $3.1 \; m/s$ has the interpretation

$$(t_0 = t \; \& \; v(t) = 3.1 \; m/s)$$

and by the logic of identity we then infer

$$v(t_0) = 3.1 \; m/s.$$

The analysis of *to* $6.9 \; m/s$ is very similar, so that after the same sort of logical inference the interpretation is $v(t_1) = 6.9 \; m/s$. The analysis of *in 5.0 s* uses the same setup, as can be seen from the analysis given. The computation for the question posed at the end of the problem goes along the same lines. The equational computations given above are trivial, but having a program that learns this special computational semantics and its associated grammar to solve this given class of problems is not.

Our non-lexical categories are

W - for word problem (and start symbol),
EC - for equation condition,
E - for equation.

Our lexical categories are

Q_V, Q_P, Q_T, Q_A - for physical quantity of velocity, position, time, and acceleration,
R - for real number,
U_V, U_P, U_T, U_A - for physical unit of velocity, time, and acceleration.

We have as terminal symbols real numbers and units $m, s, m/s, m/s^2$, and ?. No special category is assigned to the symbols v for velocity, x for position and t, t_0, t_1 for moments of time since for present purposes it is equations we are essentially working with.

The internal language is defined by the context-free grammar in Table 7. The strong compositionality of the internal equational language is transferred in learning to the denoting parts of the natural language — English in this case.

$$
\begin{aligned}
W &\rightarrow EC \\
EC &\rightarrow EC\ EC/(E\ \&\ E)/E \\
E &\rightarrow v(t_0) = Q_V/v(t_1) = Q_V/v(t) = Q_V/\Delta v = Q_V/ \\
&\quad\ t_0 = t/t_1 = t/a(t) = Q_A \\
E &\rightarrow x(t_0) = Q_P/x(t_1) = Q_P/q = Q_T/\Delta x = Q_P/ \\
&\quad\ \Delta t = Q_T/\Delta t = q \\
Q_V &\rightarrow R\ U_V/? \\
Q_P &\rightarrow R\ U_P/? \\
Q_T &\rightarrow R\ U_T/? \\
Q_A &\rightarrow R\ U_A/? \\
U_V &\rightarrow m/s, \ldots \\
U_T &\rightarrow s, \ldots \\
U_A &\rightarrow m/s^2, \ldots
\end{aligned}
$$

TABLE 7 Internal Grammar for Uniform Motion Problems

3 Theory

Basic Notions of our Theory Everything that is learned is stored in the learner's *memory*. It consists of two parts: a working memory to hold its content for the time period of a single trial and a long-term memory to store associations of words, denotational values, associations of grammatical forms and memory traces.

The long-term memory is not empty at the beginning but has stored in it an *internal language*. In the present study this internal language is stored in memory prior to learning and does not undergo any change during learning.

Whatever gets into the memory gets there by *association*. We use this concept to establish the connection between linguistic expressions and their meanings. Here, formally association is a binary relation between discourses, words and grammatical forms, on the one hand, and their respective counterparts in the internal language, on the other hand. In the present case of physics word problems, selected terms occurring in the natural-language statement of the problem are associated to equations in the internal language. For example, the preposition *from* is ordinarily correctly associated to an initial condition such as $t = t_0$ or $x = x_0$.

In our theory of learning we make a sharp distinction between denoting words and nondenoting words. Intuitively, only denoting words should acquire associations to terms or equations of the internal language. In the example used above the numbers together with their units are denoting. And so are the prepositions *from*, *to*, and *in*. All the other words ocurring in the word problem fall into the class of nondenoting words, the indefinite article *a*, the copula *is*, the possessive pronoun *its*, the substantive *car*, the verb *accelerates*. Especially for the case of nouns and verbs this may not look very natural from the point of view of conventional intuition. We emphasize however that we do not have in mind an absolute notion of denoting. What counts as a denoting word is determined by the internal language currently used in conjunction with a set A fixing the set of expressions available for association. Since the internal language varies from one domain of application to another so does the distinction of denoting versus nondenoting. In our current application, what counts as denoting is determined solely by the austere ontology of the equational language of physics.

By the *denotational value* of a word we understand the dynamically changing probability of that word having a denotation. If this value is 1 the word is denoting and if it is 0 the word is nondenoting. The purpose of this notion is to prevent nondenoting words from entering again and again into the probabilistic association procedure. We thereby exploit the fact that nondenoting words like, e.g., *the*, *a*, and *is* have a higher frequency of occurrence and should be learned more easily than denoting words, which have less frequent occurrences. Consequently, we set the initial denotational value to be 1 for all words, for we assume no prior knowledge of which words are denoting in a given language. Denotation learning follows a linear learning model:

$$(1) \quad d_{n+1}(a) = \begin{cases} (1 - \theta)d_n(a) + \theta & \text{if } a \text{ occurs in trial } n \\ & \text{and is associated,} \\ (1 - \theta)d_n(a) & \text{if } a \text{ occurs in trial } n \\ & \text{and is not associated,} \\ d_n(a) & \text{if } a \text{ does not occur in trial } n. \end{cases}$$

From various past experiments, we set the learning parameter $\Theta = 0.03$.

To show how the computation of denotational value works, let us consider further the associations given are $from \sim t_0 = t$, $accelerates \sim t_1 = t$. Let us further assume that at the end of this trial

$$\begin{aligned} d(accelerates) &= 0.900 \\ d(from) &= 0.950 \\ d(car) &= 0.700. \end{aligned}$$

On the next trial the sentence is

A truck accelerates from 2.5 m/s.

As a result, the association of *accelerates* is broken according to Axiom 2.6 i. Using $\theta = 0.03$, as we usually do, we now have $d(accelerates) = 0.873$, $d(from) = 0.9515$, $d(car) = 0.700$. After, let us say, three more occurrences of *accelerates* without any association being formed the denotational value would be further reduced to 0.620.

The dynamical computation of denotational value continues after initial learning even when no mistakes are being made. As a consequence high-frequency words have their denotational values approach to zero rather quickly. (From a formal point of view, it is useful to define a word as *nondenoting* if its asymptotic denotational value is zero, or, more realistically, below a certain threshold.)

The purpose of our principle of *generalization* is to generate grammatical forms. For example, the phrase *from 3.1 m/s* generalizes to the grammatical form *from R U_V* where R is the category of real numbers and U_V the category of velocity units. Likewise the associated equation $(t = t_0 \ \& \ v(t_0) = 3.1 \ m/s)$ is generalized to the internal grammatical form $(t = t_0 \ \& \ v(t_0) = R \ U_V)$.

When a generalization is made, the particular word association on which it is based is stored with it in long-term memory, as the *memory trace* justifying the generalization. The memory trace maps associations of grammatical forms to sets of word associations. The memory trace of a grammatical-form association thus keeps track of those word associations that gave rise to this particular grammatical-form association. If one of the word associations in the trace of a grammatical-form association is deleted, then so is this association.

The theory that underlies our learning program is given in terms of a system of axioms (for formal details see the appendix). The full set of axioms together with a detailed explanation of each axiom can be found in Suppes et al. 1996. We begin with a general formulation, which is then made more special and technical for learning the language of physics word problems.

Background Assumptions We state informally as background assumptions two essential aspects of any language learning device. First, how is the internal representation generated by the learner of an utterance heard or read, for example, for the first time. Second, at the other end of the comprehension process, so to speak, is that of generating an internal representation of a new utterance, but one that falls within the grammar and semantics already constructed by the learner.

Both of these processes ultimately require thorough formal analysis in any complete theory, but, as will become clear later, this analysis is not necessary for our present purpose. We give only a schematic formulation here.

1. *Association by contiguity.* When a learner is presented with a verbal stimulus that it cannot interpret then it associates the stimulus

Production Rules			Grammatical-Form Associations		
W	$\rightarrow$	*a car accelerates EC.*	*a car accelerates EC.*	$\sim$	EC
EC	$\rightarrow$	$EC\ EC$	$EC\ EC'$	$\sim$	$EC\ EC'$
EC	$\rightarrow$	$(E\ E')$	$E\ E'$	$\sim$	$(E\ \&\ E')$
E	$\rightarrow$	Q_V	Q_V	$\sim$	$v(t) = Q_V$
E	$\rightarrow$	Q_T	Q_T	$\sim$	$\Delta t = Q_T$
Q_V	$\rightarrow$	$R\ U_V$	$R\ U_V$	$\sim$	$R\ U_V$
Q_T	$\rightarrow$	$R\ U_T$	$R\ U_T$	$\sim$	$R\ U_T$
E	$\rightarrow$	*from*	*from*	$\sim$	$t_0 = t$
E	$\rightarrow$	*to*	*to*	$\sim$	$t_1 = t$
E	$\rightarrow$	*in*	*in*	$\sim$	$\Delta t = t$

TABLE 8 Partial English Comprehension Grammar

to the single correct internal representation, whose structure will vary from one stimulus to another.

2. *Comprehension-and-response axiom.* If a learner is presented a verbal stimulus, then by using the associations and grammatical rules stored in long-term memory, the learner attempts to construct a semantic representation of the stimulus and respond accordingly.

Probabilistic Learning Algorithm For purposes of exposition we first describe the target state of learning, when some portion of English has already been learned. In a second step we describe how to reach this state from scratch.

If the learner has already learned enough English as to understand *A car accelerates from 3.1 m/s to 6.9 m/s in 5 s*, the learner's memory should contain (i) a semantically interpreted lexicon, (ii) a grammar of English, and (iii) a compositional semantics for that grammar like that shown in Table 8. With this memory the learner will be able to interpret the English word problem *A car accelerates from 3.1 m/s* by deriving its internal language translation $(t = t_0\ \&\ v(t) = 3.1\ m/s)$. Given a more extended grammar than the one in Table 8 the derivation of the English word problem given initially is then completely straightforward.

In the following we shall describe how the memory can reach this state by learning from examples. We distinguish two cases: either no learning has occurred or some learning has occurred already. If no learning has occurred, the memory holds at least the internal language part. Unlike the robotic learning situation there is some knowledge about the English grammar already: the memory holds real numbers and physical units together with rules introducing the appropriate categories for them:

$$Q_V \to R\ U_V \quad U_V \to m/s, ..., \quad R \to 2.1, ...,$$
$$Q_T \to R\ U_T \quad U_T \to s, ...$$

Whenever a word problem given to the learner is not understood it is presented together with its internal language representation. A pair

(2) *A car accelerates from 3.1 m/s* $\sim$ $(t = t_0$ & $v(t_0) = 3.1\ m/s)$

is formed from the English word problem and the learner's internal language counterpart.

Notice that our learning procedure does not start from scratch because it already has the real numbers and units occurring in English as part of the internal language. So the problem that remains to be solved is to find the English word to be associated to $t_0 = t$. Since there are 4 English words left, namely *a*, *car*, *accelerates*, and *from*, there are 4 possibilities to associate this equation. The learner probabilistically associates the words of the natural-language expression with the symbols of the internal-language expression. The probability that the learner associates *from* to $t_0 = t$ is only $1/4$. Let us assume this indeed happens:

(3) $$from \sim t_0 = t.$$

By a principle of generalization (Axiom 1.2) the learner derives grammatical forms for both languages and derives the association

(4) *a car accelerates* $E\ R\ U_V \sim E$ & $v(t) = R\ U_V.$

The grammatical form will be stored in conjunction with those associations upon which the generalization was made.

By a principle of form association (Axiom 1.4) this association (4) will get broken down into smaller units like this:

(5) $$Q_V \sim v(t) = Q_V$$

In the internal equational language for the physics word problems we have the derivation

(6) $$E \to v(t) = Q_V.$$

From this and (5), we infer by a principle of rule generation (Axiom 1.3) the grammatical rule

$$E \to Q_V.$$

In a similar fashion, many other grammatical rules are generated:

(7)
$$
\begin{aligned}
EC &\to E \\
E &\to v(t) = Q_V \\
Q_V &\to R\ U_V \\
W &\to a\ car\ accelerates\ EC.
\end{aligned}
$$

By a principle of factorization (Axiom 2.2) we get from (4) and (5) together with grammatical rule (xviii) more general grammatical forms:

(8) $a\ car\ accelerates\ E\ E' \sim (E\ \&\ E')$.

By a principle of filtering (Axiom 2.3) the set of grammatical forms and rules generated gets then reduced to a minimal set, e.g., (4) is replaced by the following form association:

(9) $W \sim a\ car\ accelerates\ E\ E'$.

Taking (3), (5) and (7) together, our memory will contain exactly what is needed to be able to understand part of the original word problem.

Consider now one of the cases with a wrong association hypothesized. An association that could arise with equal probability is

(10) $car \sim t_0 = t$.

By the principle of generalization (Axiom 1.2) we would now arrive at the association of the following grammatical forms:

(11) $a\ E\ accelerates\ from\ Q_V \sim (E\ \&\ v(t_0) = Q_V)$.

Assume in the next trial the word problem *A car accelerates to 3.1 m/s* would be presented to the learner. Then the learner might generate the internal representation

$(t_0 = t\ \&\ v(t) = 3.1\ m/s)$.

But this representation would be wrong since it assigns the car 3.1 m/s as its initial velocity rather than as its final velocity. Coercing the correct internal representation would result in breaking the association $car \sim t_0 = t$. The words *a*, *car*, *accelerate*, and *to* would reenter the sampling process with an equal probability to be associated to $t_1 = t$.

4   Some Results and Problems to be solved

In Figure 1 we show the mean denotational learning curve for the two nondenoting words *the* and *a* in our corpus. This curve is for an initial sample of 60 of our 105 training sentences based on 100 runs of 300 trials each. The computation for this learning curve is derived from the linear learning model defined in (1).

Note that by the end of the 300 trials, — halfway between 14 and 16 on the coordinates of the abscissa —, the denotational value of the two words is close to 0.1, and the denotational value of the denoting words remains close to 1.0, which was the initial denotational value, $d_1(w)$, for all words. A much more detailed treatment of the concept of denotational value is given in Suppes and Liang 1996.

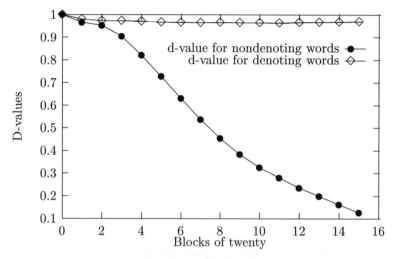

FIGURE 1   Mean learning curves for 60 English word problems.

We conclude with showing our equational analysis for two word problems that would require extension, but obvious ones, of the internal language and the English comprehension grammar given here. We do not discuss methods for actually solving these additional kinds of problems but computationally this is an easy task.

1. *Bob's car starts from rest and in 6.6 s has a velocity of 100 km/h. What is its average acceleration?*

   $(t_0 = t$ & $v(t) = 0)$
   $\Delta t = 6.6$ s
   $(t_1 = t$ & $v(t) = 100$ km/h$)$
   $a = ?$

2. *Bob's car is now traveling east at 80 km/h and 1 km to the east, Susan's car is traveling west at 90 km/h on the same road. When will they pass each other?*

   $(t_0 = t$ & $v_b(t) = 80$ *km/h* & $x_s(t) - x_b(t) = 1$ *km* & $v_s(t) = -90$ *km/h*$)$
   $(t_1 = t$ & $x_b(t) = x_s(t)$ & $t_1 - t_0 = ?)$

There is a big difference between our robotic learning experiment and the physics learning experiment. In the robotic experiment the natural language used was simple, consisting mainly of commands to manipulate an object of a limited environment in the robot's perceptual field. On the other hand, the notions involved (objects, properties, spatial relations, actions) had largely been left undetermined. In the case of physics word problems just the opposite is the case: all the notions involved can be given a rigorous definition, but the language of word problems is much richer in variety of expression with respect to contextual interpretation and anaphora.

Our learning program certainly does not reflect the approach of a human learner. For which human learner would it make sense after all to learn a language from physics text books? However, we would like to draw attention to a phenomenon that has been observed with students familiar with the physical theory underlying the word problem but not deeply familiar with the language in which the problem is presented: they generally have not much difficulty in understanding and solving these problems. For the same reason we expect our project to succeed: in that respect we think our program resembles the student who is in command of physics but not in good command of the language to be learned. We therefore conjecture that their language learning does not depend on compositionality but resembles more the learning of a fixed list of words and phrases. These phrases refer to certain qualitative notions like distance, duration, speed, acceleration. We therefore are currently developing a qualitative semantics of physical processes that fits more closely the structure of natural language than does the equational language of physics.

References

Larkin, Jill. 1983. The Role of Problem Representation in Physics. In *Mental Models*, ed. Dedre Gentner and Albert L. Stevens. 75–98. Lawrence Erlbaum.

Suppes, Patrick, Michael Böttner, and Lin Liang. 1995. Comprehension grammars generated from machine learning of natural languages. *Machine Learning* 19:133–152.

Suppes, Patrick, Michael Böttner, and Lin Liang. 1996. Machine Learning Comprehension Grammars for Ten Languages. *Computational Linguistics* 22(3):329–350.

Suppes, Patrick, Michael Böttner, Lin Liang, and Ray Ravaglia. 1995. Machine Learning of Natural Language: Problems and Prospects. In *WOFCAI 95. Proceedings of the Second World Conference on the Fundamentals of Artificial Intelligence*, ed. Michael de Glas and Z. Pawlak, 511–525. Paris. Angkor.

Suppes, Patrick, and Lin Liang. 1996. Probabilistic association and denotation in machine learning of natural language. In *Computational Learning and Probabilistic Reasoning*, ed. A. Gammerman. 87–100. John Wiley & Sons Ltd.

Suppes, Patrick, Lin Liang, and Michael Böttner. 1992. Complexity issues in robotic machine learning of natural language. In *Modeling Complexity Phenomena*, ed. Lui Lam and Vladimir Naroditsky. 102–127. Springer.

Appendix

Axioms of Learning

1. Computations using Working Memory

1.1 ***Probabilistic Association.*** On any trial, let s be associated to σ, let a be in the set of words of s not associated to any internal expression of σ, and let A be the set of expressions of the internal language made available for association and let α be in A but not currently associated with any word of s. Then pairs (a, α) are sampled, possibly using the current denotational value, and associated, i.e. $a \sim \alpha$.

1.2 ***Form Generalization.*** If $g(g_i') \sim \gamma(\gamma_i')$, $g_i' \sim \gamma_i'$, and γ' is derivable from X, then $g(X_i) \sim \gamma(X_i)$, where i is the index of occurrence.

1.3 ***Grammar − Rule Generation.*** If $g \sim \gamma$ and γ is derivable from X, then $X \to g$.

1.4 ***Form Association.*** If $g(g') \sim \gamma(\gamma')$ and g' and γ' have the corresponding indexed categories, then $g' \sim \gamma'$.

1.5 ***Form Specification.*** If $g(X_i) \sim \gamma(X_i)$, $g' \sim \gamma'$, and γ is derivable from X, then $g(g_i') \sim \gamma(\gamma_i')$.

1.6 ***Content Deletion.*** The content of working memory is deleted at the end of each trial.

2. Changes in State of Long-term Memory

2.1 ***Denotational Value Computation.*** If at the end of trial n a word a in the presented verbal stimulus is associated with some internal expression α, then $d(a)$, the denotational value of a increases and if a is not so associated $d(a)$ decreases. Moreover, if a word a does not occur on a trial, then $d(a)$ stays the same unless the association of a to an internal expression α is broken on the trial, in which case $d(a)$ decreases.

2.2 ***Form Factorization.*** If $g \sim \gamma$ and g' is a substring of g that is already in long-term memory and g' and γ' are derivable from X, then g and γ are reduced to $g(X)$ and $\gamma(X)$. Also $g(X) \sim \gamma(X)$ is stored in long-term memory, as is the corresponding grammatical rule generated by Axiom 1.4.

2.3 **Form Filtering.** Associations and grammatical rules are removed from long-term memory at any time if they can be generated.

2.4 **Congruence Computation.** If w is a substring of g, w' is a substring of g' and they are such that

   i. $g \sim \gamma$ and $g' \sim \gamma$,

   ii. g' differs from g only in the occurrence of w' in place of w,

   iii. w and w' contain no words of high denotational value,

then $w' \approx w$ and the congruence is stored in long-term memory.

2.5 **Formation of Memory Trace.** The first time a form generalization, grammatical rule or congruence is formed, the word associations on which the generalization, grammatical rule or congruence is based are stored with it in long-term memory.

2.6 **Deletion of Associations.**

   i. When a word in a sentence is given a new association, any prior association of that word is deleted from long-term memory.

   ii. If $a \sim \alpha$ at the beginning of a trial, a appears in the utterance s given on that trial but α does not appear in the internal representation σ of s, then the association $a \sim \alpha$ is deleted from long-term memory.

   iii. If no internal representation is generated from the occurrence of a sentence s, σ is then given as the correct internal representation, and there are several words in s associated to an internal expression α of σ such that the number of occurrences of these words is greater than the number of occurrences of α in σ, then these associations are deleted.

2.7 **Deletion of Form Association or Grammatical Rule.** If $a \sim \alpha$ is deleted, then any form generalization, grammatical rule or congruence for which $a \sim \alpha$ is a memory trace is also deleted from long-term memory.

Index